# HISTORY of the ORGANIZATION of CHINESE AMERICAN WOMEN 1977–2009

# HISTORY of the ORGANIZATION of CHINESE AMERICAN WOMEN 1977-2009

Compiled and edited by
**Pauline W. Tsui**

Project Director
**Genevieve Puanani Woo**

THE RUTH H. KUO AND
RHODA HOW MEMORIAL FUND OF
THE COMMUNITY FOUNDATION FOR
THE NATIONAL CAPITAL REGION
WASHINGTON D.C.

Printed in the United States of America

18 17 16 15 14 13 6 5 4 3 2 1

**Library of Congress Cataloging-in-Publication Data**

Tsui, Pauline W., compiler, editor of compilation.
History of the Organization of Chinese American Women, 1977–2009 / compiled and edited by Pauline W. Tsui ; Genevieve Puanani Woo, project director.
pages cm
Includes bibliographical references.
ISBN 978-0-8248-3897-3 (alk. paper)
1. Organization of Chinese American Women—History. I. Woo, Genevieve Puanani. II. Title.
E184.C5T8357 2013
305.48'8951073—dc23
2013010883

This book is printed on acid-free paper and meets the guidelines for permanence and durability of the Council on Library Resources.

Designed by Wanda China

Printed by Sheridan Books, Inc.

Except where noted, all photos courtesy of OCAW photo collection.

*We dedicate this book*
*to all those who believed in*
*and contributed to the cause of the*
*Organization of Chinese American Women.*

# Contents

# FOREWORD

I came of age in the sixties after immigrating to America at the age of nine as a Chinese refugee. As part of the baby boomer generation, I was caught up in the decade that marked a defining moment in American history. Everything changed in the sixties. The civil rights, antiwar, countercultural, and women's movements raised national consciousness of America's injustices and started us down the road toward greater fairness and equality for all.

I was inspired by what happened in that remarkable era. As a student at the University of California–Berkeley, I saw the Free Speech Movement ignite nonviolent student activism across the country. I was speaking about racism and sexism at a junior high school in Oakland when President John F. Kennedy's assassination was announced. I still remember Washington burning during the riots after Martin Luther King's assassination. And the escalation of the Vietnam War took me to the streets in my first protest, marching with my husband among 2 million others in the Vietnam Moratorium.

Like many Americans at the time, I felt a rising sense of social conscience—that millions of people of color, including Asian and other disadvantaged groups, were being left behind. Deep cultural changes were also altering the role of women in American society. In 1963, Betty Friedan unleashed the contemporary women's movement with the publication of *The Feminine Mystique*, her critique of the role of women in society. Her book begins with an introduction describing what Friedan called "the problem that has no name"—the widespread unhappiness of women of that period. With the founding of the National Organization of Women in 1966, equal rights for women became a rallying cry for feminists, inspiring political action that continues to change women's lives today. From politics to business to academics to sports, women have gained positions of prominence that would have been unimaginable to earlier generations.

During this period of changing gender roles and clashing cultures, Pauline Tsui and I had a cup of tea to discuss the new possibilities opening before us and the new challenges we were facing as Chinese American women. We were enjoying the hard-won successes in our careers but found ourselves missing a larger part of ourselves—a community of Chinese American women who could draw mutual strength and support from each other. We had a vision of bringing together Chinese American women to support our causes, struggles, and successes, just as we were supporting each other. Ultimately, it would be a place where Asian American women could learn, advocate, and work together, ensuring that the potential and ambitions of Asian American women did not die within the rigid confines of traditional Chinese and American cultures.

Pauline and I turned our vision into reality through the Organization of Chinese American Women (OCAW). We founded OCAW in 1977, with Pauline as its first president and with the enthusiastic support from women in the community. At the time I had just left the U.S. Senate, where I was one of a few women committee staffers, to become the highest ranking Asian American at the International Communication Agency, better known as the U.S. Information Agency. You cannot imagine how lonely it was to be a Chinese American and a woman in diplomacy in the seventies.

Despite the progress made through the Civil Rights and Women's Movements, it remained difficult for Asian American women to break professional barriers and stereotypes in the seventies. We suffered what I call "double jeopardy." Asian American women were confronting sex-role stereotyping and discrimination not only in the American society in which we lived but also in the cultures of our ethnic heritage. But women, especially Asian American women, can do anything that we set our minds to. And working with the women of OCAW, I was prepared when I became the first Asian American ambassador in U.S. history.

This book chronicles a turning point in the history of Chinese American women leaders, when many prominent and talented women from the Chinese community actively joined together to show their worth under the auspices of one organization. OCAW was a pioneer. At the time of its founding, there had never been a comparable organization for the Chinese or Asian American community. In the following pages, you will discover a succession of enterprising, energetic, and committed women who have led OCAW since its inception, role models for today's young women. You will learn the contributions that OCAW has made over the years in providing educational and social services to the community, as well as offering a focal point for networking for Asian American women.

OCAW is proud to have been a part of the progress that Asian American women have achieved, but there is still much to be done. OCAW's work is not yet finished because Asian American women still need opportunities to convene, talk to each other, share common problems, learn from each other, and leverage our collective strengths to break the bamboo ceiling once and for all.

I hope this story inspires you, our reader, with confidence to lead your community in solving its problems—however seemingly small or overwhelmingly large—and to be proactive in all your endeavors.

Ambassador Julia Chang Bloch
Washington, D.C.
June 2012

# Foreword

## OCAW: Continuing the Legacy

As you may know, the Organization of Chinese American Women (OCAW) was cofounded by Pauline W. Tsui and Julia Chang Bloch over thirty years ago. But OCAW has a proud history that new members may not know. For example, OCAW members include the following:

- The Honorable Julia Chang Bloch, the first United States ambassador of Chinese descent;
- The Honorable Elaine Chao, the first United States cabinet secretary; and
- Lily K. Lai, Ph.D., vice-president of International Affairs for AT&T.

Yes, OCAW's members include leaders from both the public and private sectors, but most of all, OCAW represents a group of women committed to promoting the success of all Chinese American women in America.

In the early years, the focus was on enhancing our leadership skills, creating role models, and economic opportunities. OCAW held training sessions designed to help mainstream women into professional careers that would provide financial stability for their families. After three decades, the barriers we once faced have been lessened.

As OCAW enters this next era, the challenges are still daunting. This is a time when our culture has been globalized. Our family traditions, obligations, and responsibilities are being redefined. We may not be financially dependent upon our children, but we still have emotional ties that are being challenged by the geographic and career pressures confronting our children. Also, many of us are just beginning to understand the clash of expectations with our aging parents and the need to confront our own issues of aging and retiring gracefully.

So, while we have made much progress, the opportunities for OCAW are just becoming more complicated and interesting. I am confident that the current national president and board are up to the task and that they will continue to build upon this great legacy.

Faith Lee Breen, Ph.D.
Metropolitan Washington, D.C.
June 2012

# Foreword

## A Journey of a Thousand Miles

A journey of a thousand miles begins with a single step.
—Lao-tzu, *The Way of Lao-tzu*

I am a child of history and heritage. I have always wanted my family's experiences and those like mine to be appreciated as part of the Asian Pacific American culture. This dream found its birthplace here in the heartland of the South, in Virginia, where the dynamics of an era began that catapulted the restless Asian women to the forefront to shape an identity not yet fully discovered, not yet developed, not yet known, and not yet understood. The two-hundredth anniversary of America forgot us. The bicentennial celebrated someone else's history, not ours.

Influenced by my grandfather's pioneering effort in building the railroad, his murder during a time of racial strife, and the challenges faced by my parents, I created the idea for a proclamation that gave us the identity and recognition that we richly deserve. I traveled throughout the United States to tell my story. With the support of hundreds of other groups, OCAW and OCA together joined me in a national effort to walk the halls of government in Virginia, the Congress, and the White House to have our history accepted as an integral part of the making of our nation. We now have in perpetuity Asian Pacific American Heritage Month, annually proclaimed and celebrated during the month of May throughout the United States. This was nearly a twenty-year project, initiated by Chairman Jack Herrity of Fairfax County, Virginia; then later introduced in the U.S. House by Congressmen Frank Horton and Norman Y. Mineta and in the U.S. Senate by Senator Hayakawa of California and our special friend, Senator Hiram L. Fong, as well as Senators Inouye, Matsunaga, and Akaka, all of Hawai'i; and proclaimed by Presidents Carter, Reagan, G.H.Bush, Clinton, G.W.Bush, and Obama.

OCAW's scope and boundaries were broadened through events that for the first time saluted international and extraordinary women: Kultida Woods as OCAW's first International Mother, who was accompanied by her husband Earl and golf phenomenon son, Tiger; and Singapore's Ambassador Chan Heng Chee as OCAW's first International Woman. Additionally, Hong Kong commissioners Kenneth Pang and Jacqueline Willis became our nexus to Hong Kong. Our extended outreach also included Xu Erwen, the first woman consulate general from China to the United States in Houston, and her husband, a current Chinese ambassador. Through the Tiger Woods Foundation, OCAW also awarded scholarships that were targeted for young impoverished girls in Gansu Province, China.

Now that we have an Asian Pacific American Heritage Month in the United States, the next step is to have our heritage celebrated in the north in Canada and south in Mexico and in Central and South America. Our contributions can grow from strength to strength and from continent to continent. Our heritage celebration will become the world's largest acknowledgment of the Asian Pacific Americans in the Americas.

The struggle continues. We have not finished. We have, however, made strides against the injustices that still remain. Julia Chang Bloch became a U.S. ambassador; Pauline W. Tsui started OCAW; Elaine Chao became the secretary of labor; Iris Chang wrote about the massacres in Nanjing; Lisa See gave us *The Secret Fan,* a story of the first language, "Nushu," written for and by Chinese women; Cynthia Chin-Lee's book, *A is for Asia,* became one of the most important readings for children in the twentieth century; Faith Lee Breen came along with me to embrace the billion-dollar Gates Millennium Scholarship Program; Anna Chennault, a Flying Tigers Airline executive, inspired generations of us to serve America; and I created a national APA Heritage Month in the United States that has become a significant outgrowth of our leadership and educational development destined to be recognized and observed far beyond our borders. And now my community involvement with Fairfax County has come full circle. In 2011, as a result of my community service, Supervisor Pat Herrity selected me to be "Lady Fairfax," the area for which I now represent more than a million constituents, both women and girls, and men too, as the chair of the Fairfax County Commission for Women.

Thank you OCAW and OCA for the support in bringing our heritage to the Americas. It was born here in America. My deep appreciation also goes to my husband, Robert, my parents, and my family, Lai, Lillian,

Shat, Leah, and my two "dogters" Jasmine and Jade. You have been by my side throughout the entire journey. And yes, thanks to my grandfather, M.Y. Lee, who crossed the centuries and whose death changed history.

Let's salute the new OCAW—Christina Wong and Christina Chang—another page in our legacy has begun.

Jeanie Fong Lee Jew (Lee Mei Hor)
Fairfax, Virginia
July 2012

## Preface and Acknowledgments

Originally, my promise to Faith Lee Breen and others was a simple listing of OCAW's thirty-two years of programs and activities, for which my own collection of records would have sufficed, but certainly not for a book. To my relief, this insufficiency is now more than made up by the contributions of all the guest writers. The fact that these writers were personally present at these events or in their own way were deeply connected recaptures details forgotten, as well as the energy and vibrancy experienced then. To them, I wish to express my heartfelt thanks. The concept of OCAW's history, 1977–2009, in this book format with multiple writers was due to Puanani Woo, project director and writer, after consultation with several writers on the history of the Chinese in Hawai'i and with Lucille C. Aono, production editor, University of Hawai'i Press.

In recollection, OCAW's early participation in the women's movement was timely for a Chinese American women's organization to be awarded a major grant from the U.S. Department of Education, Women's Educational Equity Act Program, funded under Title IX of the Educational Amendment of 1972 that prohibited sex discrimination in federally assisted programs. We acknowledge Dr. Leslie Wolfe, then director of that program, for encouraging OCAW to apply for a three-year grant entitled "Chinese American Women Educational Equity Program" from fall 1980 through 1983. With that sizable funding, OCAW was able to convene an educational advisory committee of some of the best minds among knowledgeable Chinese American women. These advisors helped to develop a substantive framework for OCAW's four training conferences in four cities across the United States and in building three training models for professional, nonprofessional, and teenage Chinese American women.

The by-products of the above training conferences were the establishment of four OCAW chapters in Houston, New York, Los Angeles, and

Maryland and a trajectory for OCAW's development. For three decades, as founding president, executive director, and acting executive director, I adhered closely to OCAW's mission and the direction set up by the advisors. With successive highly capable national presidents and working boards, we diligently worked to fulfill most of OCAW's formidable goals.

No organization can get started without strong support. Both Julia Chang Bloch and I were fortunate to have the full support from our husbands. From 1986 through 1994, Stuart M. Bloch, Esq., provided free office space for OCAW whenever we did not have a grant to fund it. After 1994, Teresa and David Ma helped OCAW to obtain an operational grant from the Herman Lissner Foundation. We deeply appreciate their eight years of efforts so that OCAW could rent a spacious and subway-accessible office in Bethesda, Maryland, with rooms for conferences and for conducting career development training classes.

My late husband, T.L.Tsui, was instrumental in obtaining the support of Congressman Paul B. Simon of Illinois in inserting the establishment of the newly founded Chinese American women's organization and its statement on "Problems and Issues Facing Chinese American Women" in the March 8, 1979, *Congressional Record.* Most importantly, Congressman Simon added a strong request for federal employment agencies to rectify the imbalance in employment of Chinese American women.

T.L. continued to assist me in applying for successive OCAW grants and in publicizing our new organization. Congresswoman Geraldine Ferraro, who was a national candidate for vice-president in 1984, invited me to her office to discuss the formation of OCAW. She firmly believed that Italian American women should do the same, too.

In 1990, responding to requests from members of the Los Angeles and Silicon Valley chapters, OCAW established an annual Presidential Classroom Scholarship Program. Its funding was from the Ruth H. Kuo Scholarship Fund and the T.L.Tsui Memorial Scholarship Fund. This program was discontinued at the end of 2008. The program provided many high school students who were children of OCAW members one week in the nation's capital to learn U.S. political processes, as well as having an opportunity to exchange ideas with their outstanding peers from around the country. It helped tremendously in broadening the horizons of our youths.

In helping the neediest of the needy, OCAW partnered in 1998 with the Education and Science Society in Virginia to provide annual scholarships to middle school girls in rural China. For seventeen years, this program helped about eight hundred girls in ten of China's provinces. OCAW members and chapters jump-started this program, which was later sustained by multiyear funding from the Tiger Woods Foundation, Mc-

Groddy Family Foundation, Mr. and Mrs. Y.H.Wu Memorial Scholarships, and the Ruth H. Kuo Memorial Fund. The Alpha Beta Kappa International Honorary Organization for Women Educators and the F.F. Fraternity participated in shorter-term fundraising efforts.

From 1993 through 2009, OCAW supported the International Young Artists Piano Competition Awards, funded by the Gertrude C. Ho Memorial Fund and the Sarah K. Woo Memorial Fund.

From 1991 through 2009, with Muriel Hom's efforts, OCAW received an annual Li Foundation of California donation for OCAW's scholarships to young accomplished artists in music; the production of ten classical operas at the Lisner Auditorium in Washington, D.C.; and seven operatic concerts at the Music Center at Strathmore in Bethesda, Maryland. Those long-term partnerships with various organizations enabled OCAW to broaden its networking horizon.

Additionally, OCAW is grateful for the generous support of the AT&T Foundation, Pitney Bowes, and U.S. West International.

Another major OCAW mission was to integrate Chinese American women into the mainstream of women's activities and programs. Its importance can be illustrated by the remarks of the first African American congresswoman, Shirley Chisholm, when she said that although she was addressed as the "Honorable" in New York, when she stepped down from a train in the South, she was still "honey."

In 1998, Christiana Chiang initiated our annual OCAW Salute to Mothers Banquet at a Hyatt Regency hotel in Virginia. It later grew into a major annual national/global awards gala under the leadership of Jeanie Jew. At those events, besides honoring its own outstanding members, OCAW honored Iris Chang, author of the best seller, *Rape of Nanking;* Kultida Woods, mother of Master Golf Champion Tiger Woods, who with his father also attended the dinner; Senator and Mrs. Paul B. Simon; Senator and Mrs. Hiram L. Fong of Hawai'i; and Ambassador Chan Heng Chee of Singapore, who cosponsored OCAW's Twenty-Third Anniversary Celebration at the Singapore Embassy on May 13, 2000.

OCAW's Twentieth Anniversary National Conference was held at the Rayburn House Office Building of the United States, April 25-27, 1997. White House briefings were part of three national conferences.

In 2001, with the help of Robert Jew, OCAW honored Lisa See, author, and Beulah Quo, actress and founder of the East-West Players of Los Angeles, at the National Archives and Record Administration in Washington, D.C. This event is now recorded in the National Archives.

For community services, OCAW conducted biennial national training conferences for Asian and Pacific American women and biennial general membership meetings for all its members. OCAW chapters held English classes for new immigrants and training forums for professional women. From 1987 through 1988, OCAW assisted the U.S. Immigration and Naturalization Services as an Approved Amnesty Agency in helping over one hundred illegal immigrants to apply for legalization status. In 1993, OCAW, with the Chinese American Retirement Enterprises, Inc. (CAREN), conducted a Survey of Needs for Low Income Elderly Housing and supported, for several years, CAREN's housing project in Maryland for senior Chinese Americans. In 1997, OCAW cosponsored a Family Violence Conference with the Prince Georges Community College under the direction and coordination of Faith Lee Breen, Ph.D. During May 9-13, 2005, Rosetta Lai produced an OCAW Asian American Leadership Development Program for nineteen senior-level management women sent from corporations, businesses, government agencies, and nonprofit organizations. This training was provided by the Center for Creative Leadership in Greensboro, North Carolina.

In retrospect, it was the collective dedication and commitment of OCAW's members and leaders that kept our national office on a professional business level and our mission accomplishments possible. Virginia Cheung, Esq., provided pro bono legal guidance for twenty-six years and Margaret Wu helped in the establishment of a professional accounting and reporting system for a decade, services for which I am very grateful.

After thirty-two years of history, we have had time to witness the role models that OCAW's newsletters showcased. Many have reached new career heights, such as cabinet secretary, ambassador, Fortune 100 woman, full professorships, and becoming successful entrepreneurs. I am particularly proud to see the tremendous changes our training made in the lives of OCAW's nonprofessional graduates and their families. Many of them now own their own homes and have sent their children to colleges.

Since 1977, opportunities have indeed widened for all women, including Chinese American women. However, discrimination against them still exists, and equal rights for women have not yet been achieved. In this twenty-first century, Asian and Pacific American women have to continue supporting each other and expanding their network with other women's groups. Together I am certain we will be able to see OCAW's dreams come true.

Pauline W. Tsui
Metropolitan Washington, D.C.
October 10, 2012

# INTRODUCTION

Who was Hevi Sipila (1915–2009), and what does she have to do with the founding of the Organization of Chinese American Women (OCAW)? Finnish diplomat, lawyer, and a United Nations assistant secretary-general, Sipila organized the first World Conference on Women in 1975 in Mexico City. The conference and the designation of 1975 as the International Women's Year (IWY) by the United Nations called the world's attention to the unequal status and treatment of women. The United States followed by establishing a federal women's program manager position in every federal agency, and the U.S. Congress approved funds to support that program.

The U.S. State Department initiated the first U.S. IWY Advisory Committee, and its chairperson was Dr. Ruth Bacon. Bacon invited Pauline W. Tsui and Julia Chang Bloch to join her committee as representatives of the Asian American women's group. Through this committee, Tsui and Bloch became aware of the role women's organizations could play in obtaining training funds for women. They invited Canta Pian and Anchen Lin to meet with them to explore the possibility of forming a Chinese American women's organization.

The stories that follow describe OCAW's history as a leading organization to advocate, plan, and execute programs to benefit Chinese American women, their education, and their careers. OCAW partnered with other women's programs and embraced all women and men as well. Pauline W. Tsui, the lead writer/compiler/editor for this book, and her assistant Puanani Woo, project director, gathered a group of OCAW "sisters" to record their perceptions and their experiences of OCAW.

In her own words, each contributor shares not only an OCAW program in which she was involved but also writes about her personal background and what motivated her activism. In 1975, I was a senior in high school, looking forward to a college education and career. The OCAW members—including my mother Nancy Chin-Lee and my mentor Jeanie F. Jew—would be watching and guiding me through my university days at Harvard and the East-West Center at the University of Hawai'i. OCAW members have helped me as I made decisions about my profession as a children's book author and corporate writer and manager, and they never lost faith in me even as I stumbled or made mistakes.

Each one of us stands on the shoulders of those who came before us. I am extremely grateful for everything OCAW and its members have done for me and the synergy of the OCAW connections. They have given me many opportunities to promote my work and to share what it's like to be a Chinese American professional in the American corporate world.

This book will help you get to know the diverse women who created and energized OCAW, which has boosted the education and careers of countless women. Settle back and enjoy their stories. You may be surprised by how we're all connected.

We hope this book will inspire you to understand the importance of your own values and actions and that you will, in turn, step forward in these days of globalization and do what you can to advocate for equality and fairness for all women—nay, for all.

Cynthia Chin-Lee
Lifetime OCAW member, Silicon Valley Chapter
Palo Alto, California
October 2012

Chapter 1

# Beginnings
## The 1970s

### Formal Establishment of OCAW: March 12-13, 1977

Four women—Canta Pian, Anchen Lin, Julia Chang Bloch, and Pauline W. Tsui—held a meeting and discussed at length the reasons and ways to start an organization for Chinese American women. They decided to seek additional opinions from more Chinese American women representing various geographical regions of the United States.

At that time, in the late 1970s, Tsui was a vice-president of the national group Organization of Chinese Americans (OCA). With support from OCA, headquartered in metropolitan Washington, D.C., whose founding president is K.L. Wang, Tsui was able to reach out and invite women from eleven cities across the United States to a Historic National Conference held March 12–13, 1977, at the spacious office building of Stuart M. Bloch, Esq., in Washington, D.C.

The conference agenda for the morning sessions of March 12 was as follows:

- Discussions on the desirability of forming a national organization of Chinese American women affiliated with OCA
- Drafting bylaws for a proposed national organization of Chinese American Women to be called Organization of Chinese American Women (OCAW)

The presenter in the afternoon session of March 12 was Canta Pian, director, Division of Asian American Affairs, and acting director, Office of Special Concerns, U.S. Department of Health and Human Services. She led the group in:

1976 OCAW Founding Members, *L to R:* Canta Pian, Anchen Lin, Julia Chang Bloch, Pauline W. Tsui.

- Discussions on problems and issues for Chinese American women with consideration of various groups and of different ages
- Reporting on the 1970 federal census statistics on educational and professional attainments of Chinese American women and their needs
- Discussions on public perception and media stereotyping of Chinese American women

Mary Lee Au, educator and president, L.A. Associates, Maryland, led the group in deciding on the following objectives to be accomplished in the first year of a Chinese American women's organization:

- Conduct a membership drive and fundraising activities
- Establish a talent bank
- Compile an efficient membership list
- Conduct self-development training on awareness, communications, assertiveness, presentation skills, resume writing, and interview techniques
- Network with other women's groups and share needs and accomplishments
- Engage in community service

Enthused over the planning thus far, the group decided to go forward to establish the national Organization of Chinese American Women (OCAW), and an election of national officers for this organization was the agenda for the morning session of March 13.

OCAW's historic elected inaugural Executive Board members were the following:

- President: Pauline W. Tsui, Washington, D.C.
- Vice-President for Programs: Beverley Jung, New York
- Vice-President for Membership: Margaret Lee, St. Louis, Missouri
- Vice-President for Finance: Marisa Chuang, Detroit, Michigan
- Secretary: Carolyn Mark, Washington, D.C.
- Treasurer: Judy Hom, Denver, Colorado
- Assistant Treasurer: Nancy Hwang, Maryland
- Representatives-at-Large: Julia Chang Bloch, Washington, D.C.; Mary Lee Au, Maryland; Anchen Lin, Maryland; Canta Pian, Washington, D.C.; and Margaret Sung, Maryland

Two speakers headlined the afternoon session of March 13. They were Maxine Hitchcock, special assistant to the executive director, National Commission on the Observance of International Women's Year, and Emily Taylor, president, National Association of State Commissions on the Status of Women.

Following the historic national conference that formally established OCAW, the Bylaws Committee worked diligently. The bylaws were finally completed and accepted in 1980. Two components of the bylaws are considered particularly important: Article III, Purposes, and Article IV, Membership. The five purposes (Sections 1–5 of Article III) are noted below, followed by Article IV.

> Section 1. The Organization shall promote the equal participation of Chinese American women in all aspects of life in the United States through the advancement of equal rights, responsibilities, and opportunities for all Chinese Americans;
>
> Section 2. The Organization shall establish a communication network to foster self-awareness and to raise general understanding of the special concerns and needs of Chinese American women;
>
> Section 3. The Organization shall seek and build bonds of common interest with other minority women's groups, particularly Asian American women's groups;

> Section 4. The Organization shall seek to integrate Chinese American women into mainstream women's activities and programs, both in the public and private sectors; and
>
> Section 5. The Organization shall develop a Chinese American women's agenda for action in the context of problems common to all women.
>
> Article IV. Membership. Section 1. The Charter Members of the Organization will be those individuals or groups who have contributed One Hundred Dollars ($100) or more by June 30, 1977.

With a showing of great confidence in OCAW, twenty-six individuals signed as charter members during this historic national conference. OCAW officially recognized them the following year as part of the conference proceedings in its First National Conference, held November 17-19, 1978.

The historic national conference of 1977 strongly rooted the Organization of Chinese American Women for the next thirty years, during the last quarter of the twentieth century and into the first decade or so of the twenty-first century.

OCAW is the first national Asian American women's organization in the United States.

## FIRST NATIONAL CONFERENCE: NOVEMBER 17–19, 1978

On May 15, 1978, a grant proposal prepared by Julia Chang Bloch and Canta Pian was submitted to ACTION, the U.S. agency that also controlled programs in the Peace Corps, VISTA, and Head Start. Their proposal resulted in OCAW being awarded $5,000.00 from ACTION, which enabled the organization to convene its First National Conference on November 17-19, 1978. It was another historic occasion for OCAW.

The theme of this First National Conference was "Chinese American Women in Voluntary Community Service and Leadership." It was held at the 4-H Center in Chevy Chase, Maryland, a suburb of Washington, D.C. The purpose of the conference was to provide the first steps in training participants to organize and to provide voluntary services to their communities. Conference planners wanted to bring together the national membership to learn about community needs and concerns, so they could formulate programs and seek funding and other resources to address the problems of Chinese American women.

More than 130 women from across the nation attended the conference. They included representatives from federal agencies, private organizations, and OCAW chapters. Fourteen chapters were represented. In alphabetic order, they were as follows: Baltimore; Central Virginia; Chicago; Colorado; Dayton, Ohio; Delaware; Detroit; New England; New York; Pittsburgh; Southern Alameda County, California; St. Louis, Missouri; Washington, D.C.; and Wisconsin.

The OCAW leadership was very aware of the needs of all women, not only Chinese American women.

The conference chair was Pauline W. Tsui; program directors were Julia Chang Bloch and Canta Pian; secretary, Carolyn Mark; treasurer, Nancy Hwang; and conference coordinator, Arlene Fong Craig.

The keynote speaker for the evening banquet was Patsy Takemoto Mink, national president of Americans for Democratic Action and former congresswoman of Hawai‘i. Her topic was "Asian American Women in Government and Politics." Mink was raised on a sugar plantation on the island of Maui. In 1965, she became the first Asian American woman and first woman from Hawai‘i elected to Congress. Mink was known to be an uncompromising liberal and was the driving force and principal author of the landmark law, Title IX of the Educational Amendments of 1972. Its thirty-seven-word law states, "No person in the United states shall, on the basis of sex, be excluded from participation in, be denied the benefits of, or be subjected to discrimination under any education program or activity receiving Federal financial assistance." It banned sex discrimination in schools, whether in academics or athletics.

Throughout her political career, Mink worked feverishly for education reforms to overcome gender and racial discrimination. After her death in 2002, Congress renamed the law the Patsy T. Mink Equal Opportunity in Education Act. Today it is commonly referred to as the Title IX Law.

For the record, the twenty-six individuals who signed in 1977 as OCAW charter members are officially recognized as such in the proceedings of this First National Conference of 1978. Following is a list of the charter members: Julia C. Bloch, Stuart M. Bloch, Esq., Ching-hwa P. Chang, Lotta Chi, Marisa Y. Chuang, Doreen Feng, Gertrude C. Ho, Josephine Hong, Beverley C. Jung, Liz King, Ruth H. Kuo, Mary Lee Au, Mary Lee, Helen Lee, Lou Shee Lee, Margaret Lee, Anchen Lin, Laura Lum, May Lum, Lillian Mark, Canta Pian, Gertrude Tai, Pauline W. Tsui, Louise Yang, Patricia E. Yap, and Lillian Yin.

There were four workshops that addressed major areas of concern that needed problem solving on a macro scale:

1. Workshop on Serving the Communities was moderated by Canta Pian, acting director, Division of Asian American Affairs, Department of Health, Education and Welfare.

   Panelists were Susan Au Allen, Esq., immigration specialist, Washington, D.C.; Rose Chao, executive director, Council of Asian American Women, New York City; Lily Lee Chen, director of special projects and resource development, Los Angeles County Department of Public Social Services; William Leung, executive director, Chinese Economic Development Council, Boston; Cecilia Moy Yep, executive director, Philadelphia Chinese Development Council.

2. Workshop on Organizational Skills was moderated by Julia Chang Bloch, deputy director for African Affairs, International Communications Agency.

   Panelists were Miriam Salkind, Washington representative, National Council of Jewish Women, and member, National Organization for Women; Julia Lear, past president and current chair, Public Policy Committee, Federation of Organizations for Professional Women; Susan Ahern, National Women's Political Caucus; Goldie Chu, Asian Women United, New York City.

3. Workshop on Raising Awareness: Cultural and Psychological Issues for Chinese American Women

   Session A: On Being Female and Chinese American was led by Dr. Freda Cheung, staff sociologist/psychologist, Minority Group Mental Health Program, National Institute of Mental Health.

   Session B: Assertive Training was led by Mary Lee Au, president, L. A. Associates.

4. Workshop on Raising Grants and Funds was moderated by Gladys K. Hardy, deputy director for administration, National Institute of Education.

   Panelists were Phyllis Belfore, social science analyst, Women's Action Program, HEW; Doreen Feng, minority business research and management specialist, Office of Minority Business Enterprise, U.S. Department of Commerce; Mike

> Gilbert, director, Northern Virginia Manpower Consortium; Judy Lichtman, executive director, Women's Legal Defense Fund.

The recorders for the workshops did an outstanding job. Anne Quan Uno, Investors Diversified Services, Inc., recorded Workshop 1; Carolyn Mark, secretary, OCAW, Workshop 2; Ruby Tsang, OCAW New York Chapter, and Patricia Hsieh, OCAW Baltimore Chapter, Workshop 3; and Ann Lee, attorney, Lacy and Jung, Detroit, Workshop 4.

This conference, which brought representatives together from divergent groups, was the first of its kind in the United States. Its purposes also reflected the overall purposes of OCAW:

- Integrate Chinese American women into the mainstream of women's activities and programs
- Build bonds of common interest with women's groups, both majority and minority
- Address a variety of issues and concerns of Chinese American women, and of all women, such as equal employment opportunities on both the professional and nonprofessional levels
- Overcome stereotypes, racial discrimination, and restrictive traditional beliefs
- Assist poverty-stricken recent immigrants
- Seek access to leadership and policy-making positions

Diana Lee, OCAW parliamentarian, New York City Chapter, and deputy general counsel of New York City, gave the closing remarks. This was followed by strong recommendations from attendees that this dialogue continue among all stakeholders seeking gender and racial equality for all women and men in the United States.

In December of 1978, following this First National Conference, the Honorable Sarah Weddington, President Carter's special assistant on women's concerns, met for about an hour with Canta Pian, Mary Au, Pauline W. Tsui, Julia Chang Bloch, and Carolyn Mark to discuss issues relating to Chinese American women. Weddington offered to call on the Interdepartmental Task Force on Women and request they help OCAW leadership deal with two major needs of Chinese American women: (1) technical assistance in organizational development and (2) improving research methods and understanding statistics on Chinese and other Asian American women.

December 1978, *L to R:* Canta Pian, Mary L. Au, Sarah Weddington, Esq., Pauline W. Tsui, Julia Chang Bloch, Carolyn Mark.

## OCAW Continues to Reach Out in the 1970s

OCAW continues to reach out. To make its presence known to the general public, OCAW marched down Pennsylvania Avenue in Washington, D.C., on August 26, 1977, Women's Equality Day, with hundreds of women representing organizations.

Prior to the march, OCAW's national president, Pauline W. Tsui, was invited by the White House to witness President Jimmy Carter signing the Women's Equality Day Proclamation in the Rose Garden. Following the signing, Tsui and other OCAW members valiantly marched with all other organizational leaders down Pennsylvania Avenue to the delight of cheering spectators and supporters.

In November 18–21, 1977, Tsui attended the International Women's Year Conference in Houston, Texas, as a Washington, D.C., delegate-at-large. It was the first U.S. national women's conference ever held and was attended by representatives from every state and First Lady Roslyn Carter. The Honorable Bella Abzug, congresswoman of New York, was chair of the conference. Abzug was also appointed chair of the Continuing IWY Commission for 1978. The purpose of this conference was to promote

August 1977, March on Pennsylvania Avenue, Washington, D.C., with other women's organizations, Women's Equality Day.

equality between men and women and to compile a Plan of Action to accomplish this.

In 1978 an OCAW delegation of five visited Donald Graham, publisher of the Washington Post, Washington, D.C.'s leading newspaper. The purpose of this visit with Mr. Graham and staff was to build more interest in and an understanding of the Chinese American community.

OCAW was very active in making itself seen and heard in the U.S. Senate and House in recommending changes to government agencies and policies that would improve the prospects of Asian and Pacific American women to benefit more from educational and social-oriented federal programs.

In 1978, OCAW supported the secretary of labor's program on Summer Youth Employment; Senators Darenberger, Hatfield, and Packwood's bill on Women's Economic Equity; and joined Congresswoman Schroeder and the Women's Legal Defense Fund as well as twenty other women's organizations in filing an amicus curiae brief in Weber.

November 1977, Pauline W. Tsui, a D.C. Alternate Delegate, First National Women's Conference, Houston, Texas.

In 1979, OCAW cosponsored two seminars with the Federally Employed Women's Potomac Palisade Chapter in Maryland. The two seminar topics were (1) Management Dynamics for Women in 1979 and (2) Money Dynamics for Women in 1980. Also that year, OCAW recommended several changes to the Department of Transportation concerning the Minority Business Enterprise Program.

In the *Congressional Record* dated Thursday, March 8, 1979, Vol. 125, No. 28, pages E 1014 and E 1015, Congressman Paul Simon of Illinois published an article titled "Chinese American Women Organize." In it, Simon relates his recent meeting with Pauline W. Tsui, president of the recently established Organization of Chinese American Women. Tsui presented him with a position paper entitled "Problems and Issues Facing Chinese American Women." Impressed with Tsui's presentation, Simon wrote, "I am inserting the statement in the Record for my colleagues who I believe will find their statement of interest and for the Federal employment agencies who can help to rectify the imbalance in their employment." Please see appendix 2 for the full statement.

The *Congressional Record* is a *must read* by staff in every senator's and representative's office to enable them to keep up with daily policy positions and bills in both houses.

OCAW played a key leadership advocacy role in getting the First National Asian/Pacific American Women's Conference for Educational Equity, held August 15–18, 1980, at the American University in Washington, D.C. It was funded by a grant from the U.S. Department of Education Women's Educational Equity Act Program (WEEAP).

In the *Congressional Record* dated Sunday, October 4, 1992, Vol. 138, No. 141, pages H 11278 through H 11281, Frank Horton, congressman, credits Jeanie F. Jew, with "the origin of this landmark legislation," referring to the month of May of each year as Asian/Pacific-American Heritage Month. This is the result of H.R. 5572 enacted by the Senate and House of Representatives in 1992. The genesis of this bill, influenced by Jew, began in 1977 as H.R. 540. Please see appendix 3 for the full statement.

## Chapter 2

# Growth Years
## The 1980s

### OCAW's Three-Year Federal Grant

In 1979 a proposal was prepared by Julia Chang Bloch, Canta Pian, Pauline W. Tsui, and Arlene Fong Craig, all of whom worked nights and weekends, to compete for a three-year grant to be awarded by the Women's Education Equity Act Program (WEEAP) of the U.S. Department of Education. The proposal designated Pauline W. Tsui as project director and Professor Esther Chow, Ph.D., of the American University, Washington, D.C., as principal consultant. As with all federal grant proposals, it required purposes, planning, accomplishments, names of administration and management staff, and a budget for the three-year grant period.

Finally, in 1980, OCAW was awarded the three-year grant of nearly half a million dollars by WEEAP to carry out its three-year project, the Chinese American Women Educational Equity Program. Public announcement of the grant approval was a historic and monumental moment for OCAW.

It is believed that OCAW's award of this grant was due to the renewal of support for the Women's Education Equity Act Program by leaders of women's organizations, and federal and state programs that promoted equality between men and women in education and occupational choices. Besides supporting these movements and programs, Tsui and other OCAW leaders took every opportunity to boldly speak up, in essence saying, "Regardless of educational background or socioeconomic position, regardless of whether they are professional or nonprofessional, Chinese American women have been confronted with race and sex role stereotyping that has hindered their pursuit of personal and professional fulfillment." This got the support of Dr. Leslie R. Wolfe, then director of

WEEAP, whose objective was to include educational equity for minority girls and women in the country. At the same time, Tsui and her husband introduced OCAW to Congressman Paul B. Simon and his wife, Dr. Jean Simon, who chaired the WEEAP Advisory Committee, and therefore they became very strong supporters of OCAW.

Following are the three-year grant requirements OCAW pledged to fulfill: (1) plan and execute two training models or curricula, one for professional Chinese American women and one for nonprofessional Chinese American women to help them understand how racial and sex role stereotypes have affected their lives, especially in occupational choices and career development, and to help them to empower themselves to move in and up in the world of work; and that these training models would be delivered via workshops, seminars, or in whatever grouping would work best for both their community and the workshop leaders to ensure the objectives of the training models would be achieved; (2) publish and circulate a bimonthly newsletter; (3) conduct a literature review offering a demographic profile of the current educational status and sex and/or race stereotyping of Chinese American women in education and employment; (4) complete a detailed bibliography on Chinese American women; (5) in the final year, conduct a seminar for young Chinese American women of high school age; and finally, (6) hold a national conference to provide a forum where grassroots representatives and educational policy makers can have the opportunity to discuss priorities and needs of Chinese American women, hoping the end product will be improved educational training models for Chinese American women of diverse backgrounds.

To facilitate meeting the grant requirements, OCAW established an office with full-time staff. Kwan Ming Koehler and Josephine Lo were program staff members and Cindy Yee was program support staff.

OCAW established a National Advisory Committee composed of Julia Chang Bloch, Lily Lee Chen, Freda Cheung, Ph.D., Esther Chow, Ph.D., Gladys Chang Hardy, Beverley Jung, Canta Pian, Betty Lee Sung, Ph.D., Tina Sung, Margot Wei, Gwendolyn Wong, and Esther Lee Yao, Ph.D.

*OCAW SPEAKS* is the newsletter that was created, thus fulfilling grant requirement 2. Its initial launch of two thousand copies dated October/November 1980 was a tremendous success. The logo for the newsletter was created by Nancy Hwang. She designed the horizontal parallel lines to symbolize the parallel heritages of Chinese and American of OCAW members. She felt this dual heritage was complimentary, not conflicting. The newsletter was printed and circulated into the year 2002, well beyond the end of the grant year of 1983, when the funds diminished. It served as a powerful bonding agent among the leadership and supporters of OCAW.

Next, a fifty-three-page scholarly research report. entitled "Chinese American Women: A Brief History and Bibliography," was started, consisting of socioeconomic data about Chinese American women summarized from a close review of 395 written sources. These were listed under six categories: (1) Historical References, (2) Education and Employment, (3) Social-Psychological Studies, (4) Literature and Other Resources, (5) Other Social Issues and Problems, and (6) General References.

The most important grant requirement was training models or curricula presented via workshops or seminars. They are summarized in the pages following the delightful story written by Josephine S. Lo, Esq.

## Josephine Lo, Esq.

We asked Josephine Lo, Esq.—who worked on OCAW's three-year grant in the 1980s and who is today a successful attorney—to write about her experiences with OCAW, how it may have influenced her to go into law, and to share a few early family life experiences. It is with deep pleasure that we present Lo's story.

> The 1977 journey from a Hong Kong public housing estate to my office overlooking the Washington National Cathedral has been like an improbable climb on Mount Everest. The studio apartment in which my entire family of seven lived had only 400 square feet, about one-third bigger than my office. My parents spoke no English and did not even have the chance to finish the second grade. I, their second daughter, made it up for them by obtaining three graduate degrees. They were hawkers in Hong Kong for their entire lives, whereas I can join my clients to hear President Obama speak at the Washington Hilton and to hear President Hu Jintao speak at the Great Hall of the People. Now, as a partner of a law firm with about 700 attorneys in 15 world-wide offices, I am not sure whether I have reached the peak or the plateau. I am certain, however, that I have dug my trail by standing on the shoulders of pioneering OCAW women, embracing the Chinese human values which are generic to all cultures, and seizing the opportunities abundant in America.
>
> In early 1983, thanks to the referral of Freda Cheung, then a psychologist at the National Institutes of Mental Health, I was hired by

OCAW as a project staff to join three other full-time staff members to help organize national conferences, coordinate training workshops, publish the OCAW newsletters, and write grant proposals. The job seemed to be a natural extension of my studies in counseling, education, and sociology. Our office space in Washington, D.C., was donated by Stuart M. Bloch, a real estate lawyer and the generous husband of Julia Chang Bloch. In those days, none of us had a computer and we shared one typewriter. We typed with carbon paper and were doomed if we made any typographical errors. Photocopying was an excursion. I had to put on a coat to walk around the block to Mr. Bloch's office to use his gigantic photocopy machine that resembled a sailboat.

Kwan Ming Koehler was the other project staff. She graduated from Cornell. To this day, I still covet her ability to speak and write impeccable English, although she is a foreign born Chinese. Cindy

Stuart M. Bloch, Esq., and Ambassador Julia Chang Bloch at their residence.

Yee, a 20-year-old bookkeeper, was more mature than her age and incredibly sweet. Claudine Ho, who was fluent in multiple languages, frequently traveled an hour from her home to volunteer and helped us conceive grant proposals. Bernadine was the most stylish cleaning lady I had ever met. She came every other week in a dress and a hat before changing into her work clothes. Her fashion statement taught me to take pride in whatever I do, be it ever so lofty or so humble.

Pauline Tsui, a co-founder of OCAW with Julia Chang Bloch, was my boss, mentor, and role model all in one. "Be nice to everyone because you don't know who will give you a push in your career," she advised, "and if you become successful, help others climb the ladder behind you." Pauline practiced what she preached, never uttering a mean word about anyone and always heaping praise on everyone. She also made politically correct statements, such as, "Don't say that you are Chinese, say that you are Chinese American." When asked about the secrets of her success, she beamed and whispered, "My husband T.L. cooks and never competes with me." Three decades before Anne-Marie Slaughter published her 2012 article, "Why Women Can't Have It All," in the *Atlantic* magazine, Pauline astutely observed that we needed men to be partners rather than competitors in women's arduous attempts to break cracks in the glass ceiling.

I admired the accomplished Chinese American women whom I met during OCAW's grant program. Julia Chang Bloch, named U.S. ambassador to Nepal in 1989 by President George H.W. Bush, the first Asian American, a woman, to become an ambassador, unfailingly brought enthusiasm and optimism to the boardroom. Esther Chow, a sociology professor at the American University, was remarkable for her beguiling dimples and passion for training nonprofessional women. Elaine Chao, a White House fellow then and later the secretary of the U.S. Department of Labor, radiated confidence, which I regarded as a form of ethereal beauty. Lily Lee Chen, the ebullient mayor of Monterey Park, radically altered the image of Chinese as passive and nonchalant. Lily K. Lai captivated me with the story of her transformation from humble roots to the executive rank in finance and telecommunications. These Chinese American women set a high bar for measuring my progress.

By late 1983, OCAW ran out of funding, and through Pauline's referral I was hired as a paralegal at a premier immigration law firm. My boss encouraged me to obtain a law degree and wrote a recommendation to get me into law school. I continued to work during the day as a paralegal, went to evening classes, studied late into the night and every weekend, moved with my husband to my in-laws' house to save money, and put off having children until I graduated from law school at age 31. After graduation, an adjunct law professor who was a partner at my current firm made a recommendation to land me an associate position.

I stumbled into the field of law by fate and the largess of my bosses and professor, but once I got in I offered my "blood, toil, tears and sweat." I returned to my office the day after my gall bladder surgery. When I was seven months pregnant, I realized I was bleeding while I was preparing a legal memorandum for a partner. I walked to the hospital across from my office and was confined to bed rest there for two weeks until my daughter was born prematurely. There have been countless working weekends and nights and interrupted vacations. One day the business negotiation and document drafting continued until 4 a.m. I was accustomed to being both a night owl and a morning lark.

In January 2011, when an ice and snow storm enveloped Washington and many people were stranded on the roads, I decided not to go home to make sure that I could be in my office the next day to close a transaction. The hotels around my office were fully booked and the only available room would cost $550. I was unwilling to pay for such luxury, just as a matter of Chinese frugal principles, even though my firm or my client would be willing to reimburse me. Thus I took a shower at my office gym and slept on a bench in my office. This physical strain on my job, however, paled in comparison with the emotional wound inflicted by a client's four-letter word for a problem that I did not create. I had to run out to the street to chill in a puddle of tears. Yet I have never looked back to ask whether the triumphs are worth the torments. It is a futile question because I cannot turn back the clock. The only way that I know is to give my calling my all.

Throughout the three decades of my career, the overarching principles that have propelled me may be distilled into three Chinese canons:

*Diligence compensates for defects.*
*Set the bar one notch beyond your reach.*
*It's not all about me.*

As a mother, I must be the kind of person that I want my daughters to be and live up to my cherished virtues. Perceived as Chinese,

I have 5,000 years of tradition and reputation to uphold. As a woman, I am obligated to provide support, access, and guidance to younger women so that the path is less daunting for them. Writing my story has awakened me to the privileges I have enjoyed and of my responsibility to pass them forward.

As a coda to my story, let me quote two of my heroines. In a January 2012 interview by the *Washington Post*, Meryl Streep said that her epitaph could be "She tried really hard." I felt as if she spoke for me. Hillary Rodham Clinton summed up my convictions in her 2008 speech: "In America there is no chasm too deep, no barrier too great, and no ceiling too high, for all who work hard, never back down, always keep going, have faith in God, in our country, and each other.

## 1981: One Conference and a Series of Training classes

The rousing Conference for Professional Chinese American Women, June 6–7, 1981, was held at the American University, Washington, D.C. It was entitled "Emerging Chinese and Asian American Women: Self-Realization and Career Fulfillment." Approximately 120 women from sixteen cities attended this conference.

Eighteen OCAW chapters plus one OCAW provisional chapter were represented at the conference: Alameda County, California; Baltimore; Central Virginia; Chicago; Dayton, Ohio; Delaware; Denver; Detroit; Houston; Los Angeles; New England; New Jersey; New York; Pittsburgh; St. Louis; Washington, D.C.; Westchester, Wisconsin; and Northern Virginia, provisional.

Workshop titles were as follows:

- Self-assessment and Image Building
- Stereotypes and Occupational Tracking
- Moving In: Career Choice and Counseling
- Moving Beyond: Career Change, Development and Employee Rights
- Job Seeking Skills: Skills Assessment, Job Hunting Techniques, Resume Writing and Interview Strategies
- Career Advancement Skills
- Untangling the Tangled Vines: Managing Multiple Roles
- Working Your Way Up

Professor Betty Lee Sung was the keynote speaker. She is highly respected for the research that resulted in her book, *The Story of the Chinese in America* (1967). The contents of this book opened scholarly America to seriously studying the lives not only of the immigrant European families that composed America but to take a look at the Asian immigrant experiences in America as Americans.

The conference program directors were Julia Chang Bloch, Arlene Fong Craig, Esther Chow, and Pauline W. Tsui.

Soon after this conference, OCAW embarked on its next Conference for Non-professional Chinese American Women, June 20–July 2, 1981, a first for these women, who were recent immigrants.

The workshops were advertised as "Job Advancement Workshops for Emerging Chinese and Asian Women," June 20, 23, 25, 27, 30, and July 2, 1981, at the Chinese Community Church in Washington, D.C.

Of the forty-five interested women for this program, thirty-five of them attended the entire series of six workshops. Their ages ranged from twenty-five to sixty, and their educational background varied from sixth grade to some college. Most were homemakers. Some had unskilled blue collar jobs and some were formerly in the professions or highly skilled and unemployed. The entire program was written in both Chinese and English. The fee for the workshops was $5.00, which contributed to the cost of providing workshop materials and a closing dinner. Upon completion of the workshops, each of the thirty-five participants who attended all six workshops was awarded a certificate and assisted in finding a job. Child care and transportation were provided upon request.

Workshop titles were as follows:

- Introduction to Workshops, Cultural Differences, Women Working in the United States
- Skills Assessment, Goal Setting
- Expanding Job Options, Resume Writing
- Job Hunting Skills, Filling Out Job Applications
- Interview Techniques, Follow up Activities
- Job Maintenance Skills, Employee's Responsibilities and Fringe Benefits

## OCAW is Granted IRS 501 (C) (3) Status

On November 2, 1981, OCAW was incorporated with the Washington, D.C., Office of Deeds as a nonprofit corporation after its office was moved to the city. OCAW's application to the Internal Revenue Service for the status as a 501 (C) (3) organization was granted on January 13, 1987. OCAW's affiliation with OCA ended in that year.

## 1982: Two Conferences and One Series of Training Classes

March 6, 1982, in Houston, Texas, was the date and site of the first field test via a seminar of the Training Model for Professional Chinese American Women that OCAW planned for and executed as part of its three-year grant. It was the very first time a conference was specifically held in the southwest region of the United States for and about Asian American women, although the conference was open to all women. More than one hundred women attended, which included Asian American and a few Black and Hispanic American women.

The Houston OCAW Chapter engaged in detailed planning for this occasion five months before the conference date. Spouses were called on to help. The logistics of planning for this conference were synchronized with the needs of the detailed professional curriculum-lesson plans of the

Houston, Texas, March 1982, Training Conference for Professional Chinese American Women, *L to R:* Esther Lee Yao, Ph.D., cochair; Pauline W. Tsui, project director; Professor Betty Lee Sung, keynote speaker; Laura Chiu, cochair.

Training Model for Professional Chinese American Women. This training model was conceived and built by a blue-ribbon committee of educators and successful Chinese American women business executives. Esther Lee Yao, Ph.D., and Laura Chiu were the conference cochairs.

The conference theme was "Emerging Chinese and Asian American Women: Self-Realization and Career Fulfillment." The conference was advertised as follows: "Its purpose is to promote awareness of broader and more diversified occupational choices and opportunities among Chinese and Asian American women. It will be beneficial to new graduates, job seekers and already employed professionals and non-professionals."

All the workshops were well attended and the moderators were very well qualified. Following is a list of the workshop titles and a brief description of each:

- Workshop I

  "Self-Assessment and Image Building" was led by Dr. Weining C. Chang. The primary concern was the role that language facility plays in performance evaluation, career advancement, and interpersonal relationships in the workplace. For the majority of attendees, English was not their first language.

  "Career Choice and Counseling" was led by Dr. Beverly Crane. She focused on the information set an individual needs in order to decide on a career.

- Workshop II

  "Job Search Strategies and Career Change" was led by Ms. Diva Garcia. As a personnel consultant and president of her own agency, Ms. Garcia emphasized the importance of professional appearance when being interviewed, the importance of writing a strong resume, and to consider how and when it's time to change careers.

- Workshop III

  "Juggling Family and Career" was moderated by Ms. Eleanor Der Bing, and the panelists were Dr. Joyce Fan, Dr. Dora Chao, Dr. Joan DeRooy, and Ms. Esther Ni. Each of the four panelists was in a different stage of family and career life, and therefore they presented varying lifestyles.

- Workshop IV

  "An Overview of Women's Legal Rights" was led by Judy Lee-Toy, Esq., and Roberta Yang, Esq. These two Houston-area attorneys presented women's legal rights from the state and federal perspectives.

- Workshop V

  "Strategies for Career Advancement" was led by Ms. Jennifer Sheffield. An important point she made was that it is OK for women to see themselves as bosses, executives, and to be in charge.

The keynote speaker was the eloquent and brilliant Professor Betty Lee Sung, Ph.D., of the Asian Studies Department, City College of New York. She provided insights into the particular kinds of hurdles or barriers, both internal and external, that emerging Asian American women—all women—must be aware of in order to advance in their careers. As a sociologist of note, Dr. Sung said that Chinese Americans have kept their problems and solutions to themselves, privately, but the "mere fact that you women showed interest in and attended this conference implies a willingness to come together and work for a common cause—to tackle problems collectively."

By all indications, this inaugural conference was very successful. The Houston area Asian American community attendees were fired up to sponsor more such conferences in their area. Regretfully, the planning committee did not compile the conference evaluation forms that were handed out mainly because so few of them were returned at the end of the conference.

The second field testing of the Training Model for Professional Chinese American Women was conducted in Los Angeles on July 10–11, 1982, at California State University. This was an ideal site for such a conference because it was close to a substantial Chinese American population center that also contained a great number of first-generation Chinese American professional women. Again, this conference was to fulfill the requirements of OCAW's three-year grant. Preplanning established the need for a two-day conference instead of one day because a large group of attendees was expected, and sure enough, over three hundred signed up for the conference.

The conference theme those two days was "Emerging Chinese and

Los Angeles, California July 1982, Training Conference for Professional Chinese American Women, *L to R:* Pauline W. Tsui, Lily Lee Chen, Linda Tsao Yang, Julia Chang Bloch, Judy Chu, Ph.D.

Asian American Women: Self-Realization and Career Fulfillment," the same theme as for the Houston, Texas, conference.

### Honorable Lily Lee Chen

Conference cochairs were the Honorable Lily Lee Chen and Judy Chu, Ph.D. We asked Ms. Chen to summarize this conference. Her report follows.

I quote from conference planners:

> This conference aims to train Chinese American women to succeed in the world of work—to acquire the skills requisite for not only career advancement but also career fulfillment. Like other minority and majority women, Chinese American women are

often barred from fully participating in the educational process and prevented from achieving their full potential in their chosen fields—they are denied the enabling opportunities.

Honorable Linda Tsao Yang, savings and loan commissioner, State of California, delivered a strongly personal and humorous keynote address. Being a Chinese American with a master's degree from Columbia University in New York, she talked about the fourteen job rejections she received from investment banking houses, so she concluded she was a double minority—a Chinese American woman and a woman trying to enter the field of finance at a time when that was unheard of.

After some discussion among conference planners, it was decided to have most of the conference in English, except for the first workshop, "Images of Chinese American Women." During the latter half of this workshop, attendees broke up in Cantonese, English, and Mandarin speaking groups.

Following are the workshops that were held:

- Workshop I

  "Images of Chinese American Women, Assessment and Image Building" was led by Ms. Beulah Quo, a prominent American actress, Phi Beta Kappa member, and community leader. Dr. Judy Chu of the UCLA Asian Studies Center moderated. Key ideas presented by Ms. Quo were that one should build a positive self-image and that being Asian American means one could utilize the strengths of both American and Asian cultures.

  "Stereotypes and Occupational Tracking" was led by Dr. Lucie Cheng, director of the UCLA Asian Studies Center. With statistics at hand, Dr. Cheng presented an interesting question for discussion: "Although Asian American women's participation in the labor force is greater than that of all U.S. women, and more Asian American women are college educated, why is their occupational status and therefore income, disproportionate to their educational attainment?"

  Ms. Lilly Lee, past president of the Los Angeles Chamber of Commerce Women's Council and president of Lilly Enterprises, was the luncheon speaker. Her topic kept the conferees listening hard, for her topic was "How to Make Your First Million."

- Workshop II

"Job Skills, Job Search Strategies" was led by Ms. Mary Wong-Lee, assistant vice-president of Allstate Savings and Loan in Glendale. Like Ms. Quo, Ms. Wong-Lee emphasized the importance of self-assessment, writing resumes well, and cautioned assertiveness in employment interviews.

"Career Advancement Skills" was led by Ms. Jennie Wong, vice-president of the Manufactures Mitsui Bank of California in Los Angeles. Ms. Wong emphasized being confident and not afraid of climbing the career ladder to higher positions with higher pay. One must be knowledgeable about the company one works for and must also improve one's skills in order to be on the competitive edge with others. She felt it important to have a mentor or two, in positions higher than the one you're in, to support your climb "up the corporate ladder."

- Workshop III

"Untangling the Tangled Vines: Managing Family and Career" was a panel discussion led by Ms. Nancy Luke, vice-president of the Chinese American CPA Society. The panelists were Ms. Feelie Lee, special assistant to the assistant vice-chancellor of student affairs (UCLA); Dr. Beverly Chu, chief physician, Alhambra Health Center, and Dr. Esther Chow, associate professor of sociology, the American University, Washington, D.C. A summary of the points they made are that women play multiple roles in society—daughter, wife, mother, career women, in-law, friend—so it is important to keep healthy, have a good support system, and learn to let others take the lead too. Women too often feel they have to "do it all themselves."

- Workshop IV

"Survival Skills, Image Building" was a topic discussed by Ms. Audrey Yamagata-Noji, counselor at Saddleback College, and Ms. Phyllis Sussman, wardrobe consultant manager for Nordstrom. Both emphasized the importance of being politely assertive and dressing professionally.

- Workshop V

  "Working Your Way Up" was a panel moderated by Dr. Esther Lee Yao, professor of multi-cultural education and developmental psychology at the University of Houston, Clear Lake City. Panelist Julia Chang Bloch, assistant administrator, Food for Peace and Voluntary Assistance Program, the Agency for International Development, who has advanced steadily in foreign affairs, an area in which many women and men have encountered tremendous barriers, advised attendees to take advantage of every opportunity, no matter how difficult, to take reasonable risks, network, and sharpen your skills in strategic long-range planning. Panelist Ms. Lily Lee Chen, city council member for Monterey Park, California, and a first-generation Chinese American woman, discussed the cultural adjustments to a new country, encouraged professional growth in one's profession, and encouraged attendees to step forward and fearlessly participate in America's political process. Panelist Ms. Sue Wong, a nationally recognized apparel designer for Cee Gee, a division of California Girl, stressed the importance of looking ahead with a clear vision of what you want to accomplish—your goals, be confident and determined to achieve them, and be guided by the values of integrity, honor, and dignity. Ms. Wong's designs saved a faltering business, and in time she opted to be owner of her own enterprise.

- Workshop VI

  "Women's Legal Rights" was moderated by Yeu-Tsu Margaret Lee, M.D., associate professor of surgery, University of Southern California, School of Medicine. The panelists were Teresa Tan, Esq., deputy attorney general, State of California; Ms. Phyllis Cheng, executive director, Commission for Sex Equity, Los Angeles Unified School District; and Ellen Ma Lee, Esq., attorney in private practice in Los Angeles. In sum, the panelists encouraged attendees to know basic employment rights of women and the avenues of redress, to know California's Title IX bill, which prohibits discrimination on the basis of sex, and to become involved in the political process at all levels.

- Wrap Up

  "Future Directions for Chinese and Asian American Women." Ms. Irene Hirano, chair of the California Commission on the Status of Women, discussed the importance of networking and that the organizations stratified along ethnic lines should join together to support each other. Ms. Canta Pian, director, Division of Asian American Affairs, U.S. Department of Health and Human Services, encouraged conferees to challenge traditional beliefs and roles that may hinder their economic development in the United States and to address the needs and concerns of refugees and newly arrived immigrant women.

From the written evaluations and verbal comments, this Los Angeles conference was a rousing success.

## The Field Testing of OCAW's Nonprofessional Training Models for Chinese American Women

The second of two training sessions for nonprofessional Chinese American women was held in the Confucius Plaza of New York's Chinatown June 1–6, 1982, and was eagerly attended by fifty Chinese and Asian American women, ages sixteen to sixty-eight. They attended two-and-a-half-hour sessions on six consecutive evenings.

The theme was "Job Advancement Workshops." The curriculum for these New York Chinatown workshops was modified to align with the perceived needs of the participants, compared to the first session of workshops held in Washington, D.C., a year earlier, during the dates of June 20, 23, 25, 27, 30,, and July 2, 1981. The Washington training theme was "Job Advancement Workshops for Emerging Chinese and Asian Women."

OCAW–New York member Beverley Jung served as program coordinator, and Diana Chen and Jennie Joe were her assistants. All three were outstanding leadership role models.

The workshop lecturer was Esther Chow, Ph.D., associate professor of sociology, the American University, Washington, D.C. Dr. Chow conducted all six workshops bilingually, in English and Cantonese. The workshops covered the following areas:

1. Needs and Self-Assessment
2. Values Clarification

3. Cross-Cultural Comparisons of Working Women in Chinese Society and in the United States
4. Expanding Nontraditional Job Options to Asian Americans and to Women
5. Job Hunting as a Problem-Solving Process
6. On-the-Job Assertiveness Training
7. On-the-Job Decision Making

## 1983: Two Conferences

The three-year federal grant also funded two conferences in 1983. The first conference was entitled "Fantasies, Realities and Challenges: Education and Career Choices for Chinese American Teenaged Women." It was held at the Mark Keppel High School in Alhambra, California, April 30–May 1, 1983, for over three hundred energetic, eager participants. The conference cochairs were Gay Wong and Charmaine Soo.

Two keynote speeches were given. The Honorable March Fong Eu, secretary of state of California, spoke about her struggles for success

Margaret Lee, *first R*, Alhambra, California, May 1983, Seminar for Young Chinese American Women, panel.

and inspiringly exhorted the audience of young Chinese American women to reach for the stars, reach for the moon, and reach for the stars beyond.

The Honorable S.Tanimoto, judge, Orange County Municipal Court, Central District, California, spoke about her persistent hard work to establish herself in the judicial system, an area in which she felt Asian American women were conspicuously absent.

The thirteen workshops were conducted by experienced adults and featured student moderators and panelists. The workshops were as follows:

1. Selecting Future Careers
2. Post-Secondary Education: What's Available
3. You're Hired: How to Land That Job
4. Financing Your Education
5. Cultural Conflicts: East vs. West
6. Breaking the Stereotype: Who We Are and What We Can Do
7. Bridging the Gap
8. Where to Go for Help: Hotline and Helplines
9. It Was a Man's World
10. Education in California and the U.S.
11. Public and Private Funding Sources
12. Generational and Cultural Conflicts and Their Resolutions
13. Methods for Obtaining Grants

The second conference of the three-year federal grant was the grand finale national conference held June 19–20, 1983, at the Executive House Hotel, Washington, D.C. This historic event hosted more than 160 individuals from a wide spectrum of professions who came from diverse geographic regions of the United States.

The conference theme was "Chinese American Women: Challenges and Opportunities in Education and Career Development." This theme reflects OCAW's primary mission of raising the bar for Chinese American women in education and occupational choices. The six workshops were as follows:

1. Handling Cultural Conflict in Education and Work

    Dr. Betty Lee Sung, professor of Asian Studies at the City College of New York, guided participants in discussion through presenting four cases on juggling family and career, social drinking, biased counseling/occupational tracking, and sexuality.

2. Bridging the Gaps

   Dr. Esther Chow, professor of sociology at American University, was the moderator and speaker for this workshop. The other two speakers were Ms. Rosetta Chen and Ms. Claudine Ho. Four gaps were identified and addressed: (1) the gap between women and men, (2) between the American-born and foreign-born, (3) between parents and children, and (4) between professionals and nonprofessionals.

3. Entrepreneurship

   The Honorable Anna Chennault, vice-chairman of the President's Export Council and president of TAC International, Inc., was the moderator and speaker for this workshop. The other speakers were the Honorable Richard L. McElheny and Ms. Rosemary Mazon. They discussed statistics showing low numbers of women entrepreneurs and encouraged women with an inclination to be reasonable risk-takers, to consider going into business for themselves as this is one mark of entrepreneurship.

4. Empowering Strategies in the Work Place

   Dr. Alice Sargent, an organization and affirmative action consultant, postulated that a good manager should be androgynous—that is, having the characteristics of both sexes.

5. Managing Midlife Crises

   Dr. Freda Cheung, deputy chief of the Center for Studies of Minority Group Mental Health, National Institute of Mental Health, described the physical, emotional, vocational, and financial aspects of midlife and offered practical ways to cope with the various changes.

6. Political Action and Participation

   The Honorable Julia Chang Bloch, assistant administrator for food for peace and voluntary assistance, Agency for International Development, moderated this panel. The panelists were Ms. Ruby Moy, Col. Kenneth Wu, Ret., and Ms. Jeanie Jew. The discussion covered the congressional process, techniques of presenting concerns to legislators, the role of political action committees, the financial cost of election campaigns, and a report on the successful lobbying of the Asian Pacific American Heritage Week Bill.

Keynote speaker Leslie Wolfe, Ph.D., director of the Women's Education Equity Act Program (WEEAP), U.S. Department of Education, complimented OCAW as a model of networking over the past three years of its grant program.

As designated project director for OCAW's three-year federal grant, Pauline W. Tsui extended her sincere appreciation to all who worked to make the previous three years meaningful for all. She summarized development of the detailed, professional curriculum and the field testing of the two training models, one for professional Chinese American women and one for nonprofessional Chinese American women. These two training models were recommended by a National Review Panel at Wellesley College Women's Research, Boston, Massachusetts, for publication and dissemination by the U.S. Department of Education.

From 2:00 to 5:00 p.m. on June 20, the last day of the conference, attendees who signed up were treated to a visit to Capitol Hill by bus to meet with their legislators who were each presented with a copy of "Chinese American Women's Issues of Concern." The issues were the following: (1) equal employment opportunities at both the professional and nonprofessional levels; (2) special needs of nonprofessional women; (3) assistance to refugees and recent women immigrants; (4) overcoming stereotypes, race and sex discrimination, and restrictive traditional beliefs; (5) underemployment; (6) income inequity; (7) biased counseling and occupational tracking; (8) occupational segregation; (9) language and communication skills; (10) access to leadership and policy-making positions; and (11) lack of statistics.

Chapter coordinators from twenty chapters were present: Alameda; Baltimore; Central Virginia; Cerritos, California; Chicago; Dayton; Denver/Boulder; Detroit; Houston; Long Island; Los Angeles; New England; New Jersey; New York; Northern Virginia; Pittsburgh; St. Louis; Washington, D.C.; Westchester; and Wisconsin. Chapter representatives actively voiced their concerns during this period of the conference. The major needs they presented were equity for women in education, occupational training and occupational choices, and that education programs should be conducted bilingually when servicing immigrants, because often English is a second language and not their primary language.

Conference chair was Pauline W. Tsui; conference consultant was Esther Chow, Ph.D.; and conference assistants were Kwan Ming Koehler, Josephine S. Lo, and Cindy Yee.

The dinner banquet held at David Lee's Empress Restaurant featured two keynote speakers. They were the Honorable Anna Chennault, vice-chairman of the U.S. President's Export Council, and the Honorable Mae Yeh, state senator from Oregon.

OCAW carried out additional nonprofessional training sessions in the areas of self-help skills in food services, catering, housekeeping, and sewing and alterations for new immigrant Chinese women from 1982 to 1988. Pauline W. Tsui wrote the proposals that were funded, and organized the projects for the training sessions. Following is a brief summary of these projects:

- 1982–1983 project funded by the U.S. Department of Labor, Women's Bureau grant for the project entitled "Self-Help Workshops for Non-Professional Women Immigrants and Refugees of Chinese Origin" (one and a half years). The training location was at the Calvary Baptist Church in Washington, D.C., and the project director, trainer, job developer, and model interviewer was Margot Wei. The number of workshop participants was twenty women. The job training program covered Chinese and non-Chinese food service skills in preparation, management, service, and entrepreneurship. The workshop topics were as follows:

1. Basic English
2. Work Attitude and Habits Conducive to American Labor Market
3. Appropriate Dress
4. Assertiveness Training
5. Worker's Rights
6. Job Hunting and Career Development
7. Planning in Job Advancement
8. Preparing for Possible Future Job Retraining and Interview Techniques
9. Job Placement

This written training program was published in 1987 by the U.S. Department of Labor as a model entitled "Job and Training in Food Service for Immigrant Entrant and Refugee Women."

## Margot Wei

We asked Margot Wei, to take us back to those weeks of training. Margot's story, written September 2012, follows.

> I was asked to write something about my experiences in "Job Skill Training for Non-Professionals." This program was funded by the U.S. Department of Labor with a $10,000 grant to OCAW in the 1980s, more than twenty-five years ago.
>
> When my husband was assigned to work at the U.S. Atomic Energy Commission (now the U.S. Department of Energy), my

1988 Skills Training in Food Service, Catering, and Housekeeping; baby-sitting offered; instructors siting, *center L to R:* Jeanette Kwok, Pauline W. Tsui, and Florence Kwok; *back row, third from L:* Margot Wei.

family and I moved to the Washington, D.C., area. I was retired from working for twenty-six years as a social worker in New York City. I had been concentrating on learning Chinese brush painting from a famous artist who was a dear friend of mine. I realized that painting is a solitary activity, and I needed to socialize with people and at the same time make some contribution to society. OCAW provided that opportunity for me.

In the late 1970s and in the 1980s there were many young Chinese and Taiwanese immigrants who came to the Washington area hoping to find jobs and meet spouses. Some had just married U.S. Chinese restaurant workers in order to come to the United States to live. Their main purpose for coming to the United States was to be able to work hard and earn enough money so that their children could get good educations and have a good life in the rich and plentiful U.S.A.

After I decided to teach, I asked Calvary Baptist Church to allow us to use one of their classrooms and their kitchen facilities without charge. Calvary is located on H and Eighth Streets, N.W., on the edge of Chinatown. It was a perfect location for this program. Almost all of the students could walk to class. For many

Margot Wei, instructor in Food Service and Catering, *left, back, in white coat,* demonstrating floral arrangements for table settings. Photo courtesy of Margot Wei.

years Calvary had been good to their Chinese neighbors, providing rooms for programs such as senior lunches, English classes, and so on.

I announced that OCAW had a U.S. Department of Labor grant to start a job skills training class. The news traveled fast, and twenty students signed up within a day. The need was so great. Many latecomers begged to be included, which was not possible.

The lessons I had prepared had to be changed soon after we had started classes. Most of the students were new immigrants, and their English language skills were very poor. I had to spend much of the time correcting their pronunciation. I could always tell from which part of China they came. I heard Cantonese English, Shanghai English, Beijing English, and so on. However, most of the students were young, and they improved quickly. They learned words and sentences related to household and food service work.

We were very lucky that the Hyatt Hotel on Tenth and H Streets had just opened, and also that the Convention Center was under construction on Ninth and H Streets, N.W. I went to visit the housekeeping and food service managers at the Hyatt Hotel and the head chef at the Convention Center. They all were very interested in our program, and eventually most of our students were hired by these two places.

At the start of our program, I warned the students that being on time for class was strictly required. They must not miss classes unless they were very ill or if they had found a job. I called every absent student to find out the reason for missing class. This was an important job skill. We also had a few dress rehearsals for mock job interviews. I felt that the practices really gave them a lot of confidence in real-life interviews.

During our program, I found out that almost all of the students had never been out of the D.C. Chinatown area. I planned trips to Longwood Gardens in Delaware, apple picking in a local orchard, and several picnics in nearby parks. I wanted them to learn a little more about the culture of America.

After a few months of teaching and leading my group, they felt that I truly cared about their welfare, and that I worked hard to get them good jobs. They then asked me to help with many other problems. My part-time job seemed to change to a full-time job. Nineteen out of twenty students got employment through this

> program. The remaining one went off to work at a brother's Tofu factory.
>
> Twenty-five or more years have gone by. I occasionally meet up with some of my students. Many have become the supervisors in hotels. I am so proud that my students were all reliable, cooperative workers who were seldom absent and always punctual for work.
>
> Many of their dreams came true. Almost all their children went to good colleges and several went to Ivy League schools. They have good lives now, and I am sure they will continue to contribute to this great country.

The "Self-help Workshops for Non-professional Women Immigrants and Refugees of Chinese Origin" was the model for the following 1984-1988 projects funded by the D.C. Private Industry Council (PIC),

- 1984 project funded by the D.C. Private Industry Council (PIC): "Self-Help Skills Training in Food Service and Catering," project director, Pauline W. Tsui; skills instruction, Margot Wei; counselors and job developers, Grace Ma and Theresa Chee (six months)
- 1984 project funded by the D.C. PIC: "Self-Help Skills Training in Food Services, Catering and Housekeeping," project director, Pauline W. Tsui; consultant and job developer, Margot Wei; instructors, Florence Kwok, Sister Molia Sieh, and Theresa Hung (six months)
- 1985 project funded by the D.C. PIC: "Self-Help Skills Training in Sewing and Alterations," project coordinator, Florence Kwok; skills trainer and fashion show producer, Yolanda Chen (six months)
- 1986 project funded by the D.C. PIC: "Self-Help Skills Training in Food Services, Catering and Housekeeping," project director, Florence Kwok; trainer, Sister Molia Sieh (six months)
- 1988 project funded by the D.C. PIC: "Self-Help Skills Training in Food Services, Catering, and Housekeeping," project director, skills trainer, and job developer, Florence Kwok; English instructor, Jeanette Kwok (six months)

In the 1985 "Training in Sewing and Alterations," in which Florence Kwok served as the project coordinator and Yolanda Chen served as skills trainer and fashion show producer, Yolanda presented her graduating class in a fashion show wearing their own creations. None of them had ever sewn a dress or anything before. Two of the graduates were placed in jobs with the Neiman Marcus Department Store, Alterations Department.

All of OCAW's training projects for nonprofessional Chinese and Asian American women were able to accomplish 100 percent placement of their students in jobs. OCAW was selected by PIC as being one of their three best grant programs.

## Florence Kwok

We asked Florence Kwok to comment on her experiences in the training programs. Her story follows.

> From 1984 to 1988, Pauline was able to get five grants from the Private Industry Council of Washington, D.C. These grants were partly funded by private sources and partly by the D.C. government. Pauline was the project director and Margot Wei taught the first classes and set up a model for the subsequent ones to follow. Those enrolled in these programs ranged in age from twenty to sixty, with various educational backgrounds. Their English level was from zero to bare minimum. They came mostly from the People's Republic of China, with a few from Hong Kong, Taiwan, and Vietnam. Each student received a stipend for their transportation expenses to attend the classes. Now, twenty-five years later, I have heard from a number of former students who have told me that their dream of giving their children the future they had hoped and worked so hard for has come true. Their children are home owners, college graduates with good jobs, and are raising their own families with pride, solidarity, and gratitude for the opportunities available to them.

In 1984, OCAW won a *Washington Post* Philip Graham Fund grant to assist continuing the publication of its newsletter, *OCAW SPEAKS.* Also in 1984, the Hong Kong and Shanghai Banking Corporation granted funds to continue OCAW's newsletter and operational funds.

From 1985 to 1996, Stuart M. Bloch's donation of rent for OCAW's national office space in Washington, D.C., was of tremendous help to OCAW.

On February 20, 1984, OCAW's National Board approved amendments to its bylaws, which were finalized by Virginia Cheung, Esq., and passed by the general membership. OCAW's legal guidance was provided pro bono by Ms. Cheung until 2009.

In 1984 Mrs. Meiching L. Kao donated one-half of the proceeds from the sale of her popular cookbook, *Chinese Cooking the Micro-Way,* to

OCAW. In subsequent years she donated dozens of her books to OCAW for fund-raising efforts.

In 1986 the *Chinese Home Cooking* cookbook, coauthored by Julia Chang Bloch and Elaine Lowe and published by Stuart M. Bloch, was donated to OCAW. Many of the recipes, which required only forty-five minutes of preparation, were favorites of OCAW members. Recipes from it were featured in the *Washington Post, Kansas Times*, and *Family Circle* magazine. This gave national prominence to OCAW, as well as to the easy-to-make family-style recipes featured. The cookbook went into a third printing.

In December 1984, the Women's Education Equity Act Program of the Department of Education awarded OCAW again with a one-year grant to conduct a program themed "Teenage Women in Concert: Overcoming Barriers in Math and Science." This project was conducted in Washington, D.C, Boston, New York, Chicago, and San Jose. At each city, OCAW held an essay contest for high school girls on the theme of "Science a Challenge: Why Science and Math Challenge Me."

An advisory committee composed of twelve female scientists and mathematicians—Asian, African, Hispanic, and white Americans—judged and selected the best essay from each racial group and presented the winners in a forum in each city. These forums were set up to promote exchanges of ideas between students, teachers, administrators, and parents to promote improved curriculum for inspiring girls to be interested in their possible future careers in math or science. The award forum locations and coordinators are listed below:

1. Metro Washington, D.C.: National Institutes of Health, girls from thirty-six metro area schools participated and the program was coordinated by Pauline W. Tsui, assisted by Daphne Kwok
2. Houston: University of Houston, coordinated by Grace Hsu
3. Chicago: University of Chicago, coordinated by Rosetta Lai
4. Boston: Boston High School, coordinated by Beatrice Lee
5. New York: New York Technical Institute, coordinated by Jane Ling Hom
6. San Jose: San Jose High School, coordinated by Ruby Tsang

On May 20, 1985, a historical first White House briefing for Asian/ Pacific American women was held by a written request from Pauline W. Tsui to the Honorable Elizabeth Paschall, White House liaison aide of the

Reagan Administration. About 250 women attended, representing Burmese, Cambodian, Chinese, Hmong, Japanese, Korean, Laotian, Filipino, Thai, Vietnamese, and Samoan descent from across the United States attended the briefing. Pauline W. Tsui represented OCAW in compiling the guest list. The speakers were Frank Castillas, assistant secretary of labor for employment and training; Bruce Chapman, deputy assistant to the president and director of the Office of Planning and Evaluation; Elaine Johnston, acting deputy director of the National Institute for Drug Abuse; Dr. David Diebold, deputy assistant secretary of commerce; Dr. Gary Bauer, undersecretary of education; Dr. Susan Koch, assistant for strategic defense and space access control policy and the Honorable Anna Chennault.

From December 6 to 8, 1985, OCAW's Fourth National Conference was held at the Marriott Hotel, Arlington, Virginia, chaired by Nancy Linn Patton. Cochair was Faith Lee Breen, Ph.D. The conference theme was "Issues and Concerns of Chinese American Women in the '80s." President and Mrs. Ronald Reagan sent their greetings to OCAW for a successful conference.

In the general session, Dr. Freda Cheung, psychologist, National Institute of Mental Health, spoke on "Social Concerns of Chinese American Women in the '80s: Achieving Personal Well-Being." Workshop titles were as follows:

1. Our Changing Families
2. Understanding Cross-Cultural Differences
3. Career Concerns of Chinese American Women in the '80s
4. Understanding Your Organization's Culture and Using It to Your Advantage
5. Finding the Entrepreneur in You
6. Women in Leadership
7. How to be an Effective Public Speaker
8. How to Get Government Appointments

The conference was preceded by a White House briefing organized by the Honorable Linda Arey, special assistant to President Reagan and deputy director for public liaison.

In 1986 OCAW supported the formation of Coalition of Minority Women in Business, Inc. OCAW recommended Linda Lee, Esq., to be the president and Pauline W. Tsui vice-president. The coalition was awarded a grant from the U.S. Department of Commerce, Minority Business Development Agency. The grant project financed one-year of training workshops covering subjects in real estate, broadcasting, international trade, health, and other topics of interest to minority businesswomen in Washington, Chicago, Miami, and Los Angeles. The grant project also promoted the contributions of minority women for their development, maintenance, and success in American business.

OCAW conducted a membership survey in 1986. A total of 1,800 copies of the questionnaire were distributed, and 202 completed forms were returned. Although the response rate was only 1.2 percent, it was broad enough in terms of geography: from Chicago to Houston, from Honolulu to Boston, age, profession, income, and so on. So it did give a sense of the diversity of the individuals who made up the membership. It sketched a portrait of a woman as follows:

1. She was an overseas-born, first-generation American
2. She went to a college or graduate school in the United States
3. She majored in a branch of the humanities, social science, or business
4. She was a career woman, probably an administrator/manager or a professional specialist, earning at least $30,000 per year
5. She owned her own house with her husband
6. She had 2.5 children
7. She voted regularly
8. To her, the priority agenda for a Chinese American organization should be devoted to dispelling stereotypes and secondly gaining better access to administrative decision-making positions and putting more Chinese Americans in elected office

In 1987–1988, OCAW was designated and trained by the U.S. Immigration and Naturalization Service to be one of its Qualified Designated Entities to assist illegal aliens to apply for legal status. This program enabled many qualified aliens as far away as Florida to seek assistance from OCAW in obtaining their preliminary permanent residence. OCAW engaged Irene M. Hui, who was fluent in Mandarin, Cantonese, and Shanghai dialects, as well as English, to be the administrative assistant and legalization counselor. The project director was Pauline W. Tsui, and project staff, Ivy Wong. Over one hundred people received help under this program.

## OCAW's 1987 Women-to-Women Exchange Program

During August of 1987, OCAW embarked on the historic Women-to-Women Exchange Program. Lily K. Lai, Ph.D., OCAW national president from 1984 to 1990, has summarized this occasion in her colorful, detailed report with pictures.

## Dr. Lily K. Lai

The Women-to-Women Exchange Program is one of the most important programs during the first thirty years of OCAW history. This section will discuss this program and its first delegation's visit to the Republic of China (Taiwan), the People's Republic of China (China), and Hong Kong in August 1987.

### Goals and Theme of the Exchange Program

With the endorsement of President and Mrs. Reagan, as well as Vice-President Bush, OCAW established the Women-to-Women Exchange Program in 1987 with women's organizations in Taiwan, China, and Hong Kong. As the first national organization of American women of Chinese descent, OCAW was in a unique position to assist in strengthening ties between the United States and Taiwan, as well as between the United States and China and Hong Kong. As Chinese American women, they bridge two cultures and can thus serve to promote better understanding, expand lines of communication, and identify areas of common interests. The primary goals of the program were (1) to establish links with national women's organizations in Taiwan, China, and Hong Kong; (2) to strengthen cultural, educational, and economic ties through personal contacts and communication with women leaders of these organizations; and (3) to develop joint projects of mutual interest. The theme of this program was "Building Bridges Because Women Care." In keeping with the theme, OCAW identified five broad issues of interest: (1) upgrading the status of women in employment; (2) increasing international business opportunities for women; (3) increasing cross-cultural educational programs; (4) facilitating economic stability and growth through greater cooperation; and (5) working toward peace.

Dr. Lily K. Lai.

## The Delegation

Participation as an OCAW delegate was by invitation of the OCAW Board. The criteria for delegate selection were community services, personal accomplishments, and geographic and age considerations. The delegation was cochaired by the Honorable Anna Chennault and Dr. Lily K. Lai. The delegation was comprised of twenty Chinese American women leaders from business, education, and public services. Each delegate introduced below is in the order of her last name (except for Chennault and Lai), and only her professional positions at the time of the trip are included.

Hon. Anna Chennault (Washington, D.C.), cochair, OCAW Delegation; president, TAC International; honorary chair, National Republican Heritage Group Council

Lily K. Lai (New Jersey), cochair, OCAW Delegation; chief financial and planning officer and vice-president of Asia/Pacific Operations, U.S. West International; national president, OCAW

Faith Lee Breen (Maryland), chair, Youth Committee of the National Republican Heritage Group Council; associate professor of economics, Prince George's Community College; vice-president, OCAW

Trudie Ball (Washington, D.C.), president, Taste of China and Empress, Inc.; president, Pacific International Trading Corporation

Linda Chen (Maryland), president, Systek International, Inc; president, OCAW Chesapeake Chapter

Rosetta Chen (Illinois), director of customer Service, Deltak Training Corporation

Diana Cheng (Texas), president, Diana Cheng & Associates; president, Chinese Chamber of Commerce of Dallas, Texas

Lungching Chiao (Virginia), senior program officer, the Center for International Education, the U.S. Department of Education; board member, Education and Science Society

Lily Liu (New York), honorary chair, Chinese Import and Export Association of America; vice-president, Dragon Gate Import and Export Company

Lisa Lu (California), actress and film producer; vice-president, International Broadcast System; president, Lisa Lu Production

Nancy Linn Patton (Washington, D.C.), marketing manager for Public Sector Group in D.C. and Montgomery County, IBM Corporation

Betty Lee Sung (New York), professor of Asian studies, City College of New York; author of eleven books and monographs

Anita Tong (Washington, D.C.), hostess, Feature & Window on the World Programs; writer, reporter, broadcaster, and producer of radio programs for Voice of America

Pauline Woo Tsui (Washington, D.C.), cofounder, OCAW, chair-designate, D.C. Commission for Asian and Pacific Islander Affairs; vice-president, Coalition of Minority Women in Business, Inc.

Sunny Hsu Van Buren (Maryland), president, International Express Manufacturer and Hunan Gourmet

Katherine Wei (New York), chair, Falcon Shipping Group and Eagle Fisheries; Gold medalist of the 1978 and 1984 World Bridge Olympics

Margot Wei (Maryland), developer, trainer, and author of *Job Training in Food Services for Immigrant, Entrant, and Refugee Women,* published by the U.S. Department of Labor for OCAW

June Tang Williamson (Maryland), computer program specialist, U.S. Department of Army

Mae Yih (Oregon), state senator, Oregon

Cecilia Yu (California), vice-president, CKY Environmental Consultants; senior engineer, Bechtel and TRW

## WHITE HOUSE BRIEFING, AUGUST 6, 1987

It was with a great pride for OCAW to inaugurate this exchange program with a special White House briefing for its first delegation on August 6, 1987. The Honorable Linda L. Arey, special assistant to the president, arranged for the briefing. It served to inform the delegation of current relationships among the United States, Taiwan, Hong Kong, and China, as well as U.S. policies in the areas of national security, trade, economics, education, and cultural exchange. Speakers at the briefing were in the following sequence:

Mr. Donald Gregg, assistant to the vice-president of the U.S.A. for national security

Mr. Roger Bolton, assistant U.S. trade representative

Mr. Douglas Paal, director of Asian affairs, National Security Council

Ms. Donna Tuttle, undersecretary of the U.S. Department of Commerce

Hon. Linda L. Arey, special assistant to the president and deputy director of the White House Office of Public Liaison

OCAW Delegation at White House Briefing arranged by Hon. Linda L. Arey, *last row, R of U.S. flag*. Photo courtesy of Dr. Lily K. Lai.

After the White House briefing, the delegation attended a banquet hosted by Mrs. Julie Chien, wife of Dr. Fu Chien, representative of the Coordination Council for North American Affairs (the highest official representative of Taiwan in the United States) at the elegant, historical Twin Oaks. This was a wonderful way to start their mission since their first stop was Taipei, Taiwan.

## TAIWAN, AUGUST 9–12, 1987

Their hosts in Taipei, Taiwan, warmly greeted the delegation on Sunday, August 9. They went on a guided tour of the National Palace Museum, which housed many outstanding works of Chinese arts and antiques from previous dynasties. Most of the treasures were moved to Taiwan from China when President Chiang Kai-shek retreated to Taiwan in 1949.

Delegation at banquet hosted by Mrs. Julie Chien, *standing*. Photo courtesy of Dr. Lily K. Lai.

The delegation held its official meetings on August 10–11. At the beginning of each meeting, the cochairs, Ms. Chennault and Dr. Lai, explained the purposes of the visit and the goals of OCAW. After the exchange of general greetings, each delegate briefly introduced herself. The meetings scheduled for the delegation in Taiwan were as follows:

***August 10***

Dr. Titania J.T. Chien, director, Department of Women's Affairs, Central Committee of the Kuomintang

Mr. David Dean, director, the American Institute in Taiwan; Mr. and Mrs. Dean hosted a luncheon for the delegation after the meeting

Dr. Jeanne Tchong Koei Li , director general, China Youth Corps

Minister Ta-hai Lee, minister of economic affairs

Dr. Yah-chuan Wang, secretary general, Chinese Women's Anti-Aggression League; Dr. Wang also hosted a dinner for the delegation after the meeting

***August 11***

Prof. Nora Lan-hung Chiang, coordinator, Women's Research Program, Population Studies Center, National Taiwan University

Delegation had a meeting with Dr. Yah-chuan Wang, Secretary-General Chinese Women's Anti-Agression League, *fourth from R, second row*, at premier's residence. Photo courtesy of Dr. Lily K. Lai.

Dr. Shirley W.Y. Kuo, deputy governor, The Central Bank of China
Mrs. Kuo Hua Yu, wife of the premier of the Republic of China
Minister Kao Wen Mao, minister of education
Mr. C.H. Lu, deputy director, Exhibition Department, Taipei World Trade Center

In addition to the official meetings, Mr. Lu gave the delegation a personal presentation and guided tour of the Taipei World Trade Center, which best demonstrated Taiwan's impressive economic growth and the fruits of its good educational and economic policies. The center, a contemporary modern building occupying the size of a city block, offered one-stop shopping of all the goods that Taiwan had to export.

***August 12***

Mr. Yu-ming Shaw, director, Government Information Office; after the official meeting, Mr. Shaw held a press conference for the del-

Delegation at meeting with Minister Kao Wen Mao, the only male, *fifth from R*. Photo courtesy of Dr. Lily K. Lai.

egation at the Grand Hotel in Taipei. Many major TV and newspaper reporters attended the press conference.

In addition to Taipei, the delegation was scheduled to tour the East-West Cross Island Highway and Taroko Gorge and visit a marble factory in Hua-lien, but these were canceled due to very tight schedule. OCAW thanks Taiwan for the warm hospitality extended to its delegation in hosting the local travel and dinners.

***Summary of Official Discussions in Taiwan***

The delegates were very impressed with Taiwan's spectacular economic growth and status of women, as well as its economic and educational policies and systems.

The delegation learned from Mr. David Dean that the relationship between the United States and Taiwan was good and that Taiwan was one of the largest trading partners of the United States. To trim its trade surplus with the United States, Taiwan had been making some major purchases, including American aircraft and high-tech

Delegation at press conference, Grand Hotel, Taipei. Photo courtesy of Dr. Lily K. Lai.

equipment. Mr. Dean had high praise for two recent policy changes by Taiwan: the easing of foreign trade restrictions and the repeal of martial law.

Minister Tai-hai Lee gave the delegation background information on the very successful land reform program and examples of various joint ventures between Taiwanese and American companies. To illustrate how Taiwan had been promoting open trade, Dr. Lee disclosed that Taiwan had lifted restrictions on the outflow of foreign exchange so that people who wished to invest up to U.S. $5 million abroad did not have to obtain government approval.

Dr. Shirley Kuo, who holds a Ph. D. in economics from the Massachusetts Institute of Technology (MIT), told us that Taiwan's economy had stayed relatively strong, in spite of two energy crises, for three main reasons. First, Taiwan had a large trade surplus. Second, Taiwan mostly imported productive goods rather than consumer or luxury goods. Third, Taiwanese manufacturers, ever sensitive to the U.S. market, were quick to switch from goods subject to quotas to those free from such restrictions. That enabled Taiwan to keep up brisk exports to the United States. Dr. Kuo added that recent appreciation of the Taiwan currency against the U.S. dollar was seen as a positive sign. Although the revaluation would make Taiwanese products relatively more expensive for Americans, it would encourage more competition and thus help to strengthen Taiwan's economy in the long run.

Minister Kao Wen Mao returned to Taiwan after having spent many years studying and teaching in American universities. His American experience gave him a special perspective on Taiwan's educational system. He spoke very frankly about the strengths and weaknesses of Taiwan's educational system, particularly focusing on the entrance examination system for middle school, high school, and college. The uniform college entrance examination determined which students could go to which colleges and in what majors based on the score of the examination and the order of the wish list each student wrote on the application form for the examination. The obvious benefit of this system was that it was equitable. The drawback was that teachers tended to teach what would help students pass the examination rather than concentrate on what was important for the future of the students. Dr. Mao realized that the educational system must achieve several social goals, and he had instituted some reforms, including the upgrading of vocational education. He emphasized that vocationally skilled workers were just as important to the economy as professional workers.

Professor Nora Chiang and her colleagues at the Population Study Center of the National Taiwan University were conducting women's research programs, and the center also published books on the status of women in the economy. Their research found two interesting trends among Taiwanese women: (1) Like American women, more women in Taiwan were holding jobs and child care was a growing problem; and (2) even though women were working outside the home, they still did most of the household chores, like their American sisters.

Another interesting observation by the delegation was that most of the women leaders the delegation met in Taiwan had Ph.D. degrees from American universities.

## HONG KONG, AUGUST 13–14, 1987

Although the delegation spent only two days in Hong Kong, they definitely made the most of them.

### *August 13*

The delegation attended a luncheon hosted by Mrs. Betty Tung and Mrs. Alice King at the beautiful Island Club, and Mrs. Anderson, wife of the U.S. consul general in Hong Kong, also joined us at the elaborate luncheon.

Mrs. Betty Tung, director, the Orient Overseas Line; managing director, Proluck Enterprises Co., Ltd.

Mrs. Alice King, daughter of the shipping magnate, C.Y. Tung; a patron of the arts in Hong Kong

After Lunch, the delegation visited Mrs. Maria Lee, president/owner and managing director of Maria's Company, specializing in baked goods. It had seventy branches in Hong Kong, Taiwan, Los Angeles, and New York. In addition to her entrepreneurial skills, Mrs. Lee is an accomplished artist, singer, poet, and writer. The delegation visited her company headquarters and her cultural center.

That evening the delegates were treated to the famous Maria pastries and a banquet on the Jumbo, the famous floating restaurant, hosted by Mrs. Lee. After dinner, the delegates had so much fun taking pictures of themselves dressed up as the Chinese emperor and his consorts.

Delegation at banquet on Jumbo hosted by Mrs. Maria Lee, *fourth from L, second row.* Photo courtesy of Dr. Lily K. Lai.

Delegation at breakfast meeting hosted by Mrs. Ng Tor Tai, *sixth from R, first row*. Photo courtesy of Dr. Lily K. Lai.

***August 14***

Mrs. Ng Tor Tai hosted a breakfast and held a press conference for the delegation. Among the guests were the following Hong Kong women leaders:

Mrs. Tor Tai Ng, managing director, Asian City Development, Inc., USA
Mrs. Pauline Ng, J.P., member of the Legislative Council
Mrs. Ko Siu Wah Kwan, J.P., YWCA general secretary; former member of legislative council
Mrs. Peggy Lam, MBE, J.P., chair, Wanchai District Council; executive director, Family Planning Association of Hong Kong
Dr. Chung Chi Yung Wu, president, Shu Yan College
Mrs. Fung Chan Heung Tao, member, Hong Kong Stock Exchange
Mrs. Vicky Leung, film producer, Pearl City Production Ltd. and Pearl City Films Ltd.
Mrs. Anita Leung, head of international and corporate affairs, Hong Kong Stock Exchange
Miss Ellen May-May Fong, musician; lecturer, the Hong Kong Music Institute
Miss Elsie Leung, solicitor

### *Summary of Official Discussions in Hong Kong*

People in Hong Kong enjoyed personal freedom and great economic success. Most of the women leaders the delegation met in Hong Kong were successful businesswomen in various lines of businesses and industries. Most of the discussions were focused on personal success stories and how their businesses were managed.

For example, Mrs. Maria Lee started out giving cooking lessons and began her first bakery with her students' encouragement. With a bank loan of HG $18,000, she was able to build her business into a HG $1.5 billion enterprise. Mrs. Lee gave a lot credit for her success to her employees, especially her able vice-president, Mrs. Fu. Mrs. Lee explained how she had instituted good management practices and a profit-sharing system for her employees.

## CHINA, AUGUST 15–21, 1987

The delegation had official activities in Shanghai and Beijing from August 15 to August 19. Fourteen of the delegates went on to Xian and Guilin after the official meetings ended in Beijing.

### *Shanghai, August 15*

Shanghai has always been a major Chinese port, so it was appropriate that the delegates entered China via that city.

The delegation visited many historical places and scenic spots in Shanghai. They spent the afternoon shopping at the China Friendship Stores. The delegates were very impressed with the variety and quality of merchandise, such as cotton and silk products, porcelains, and jade.

Some of the delegates also got their first lesson in China's monetary system. There were two different forms of currency in China: foreign exchange certificates and people money. The foreign exchange certificate was the official money foreign visitors got when they exchanged U.S. dollars or other foreign currencies for Chinese currency. This foreign exchange certificate was accepted everywhere in China and was worth more than people money for the same face value.

In the evening, the delegation attended a banquet hosted by the Shanghai Overseas Organization, China Council for Promotional Trade, Shanghai Council, and the Shanghai Branch of the China Travel Bureau. Among the guests were more than fifty prominent Shanghai women leaders. Some of the leaders are listed below:

Delegation at banquet hosted by the Shanghai Overseas Organization, China Council for Promotional Trade, Shanghai Council and Shanghai Branch of the China Travel Bureau and the Friendship Association. Photo courtesy of Dr. Lily K. Lai.

Dr. Xide Xie, president, Fudan University
Ms. Zhikang Xing, director, Shanghai Women's Federation
Mr. Jingchuan Mao, chair, Association with Foreigners
Ms. Danfeng Wang, famous movie actress
Ms. Juifang Zhang, famous stage actress

***Beijing, August 17–19***

August 17

The delegation began with a guided tour of the Forbidden City, and the delegates were struck by the richness of their ancestry. Then they went on to tour the Great Wall. For many delegates who had waited for a lifetime to be able to stand on the Great Wall, it was a dream fulfilled.

That evening the delegation was invited to a banquet at the Windows of the World Building, hosted by Ambassador Wengin Zhang, a former Chinese envoy to the United States and director of the Chinese Friendship Association. The delegates met many Chinese women leaders at the banquet.

A special cake made to welcome the OCAW delegation to Beijing at the banquet hosted by Ambassador Wengin Zhang, *second from R.* Photo courtey of Dr. Lily K. Lai.

AUGUST 18

The delegation's first official meeting in Beijing was with President Muhua Chen of the People's Bank of China.

That afternoon the delegation was welcomed by President of All China Women's Federation, Keging Kang and Vice-President Jiejiong Lei. President Kang hosted a banquet in the Beijing Room of the Great Hall of the People after the meeting. Many Chinese women leaders attended the banquet.

AUGUST 19

The delegation met with U.S. ambassador to China Winston Lord and Mrs. Bette Bao Lord at the U.S. Embassy in Beijing. After the meeting, Mrs. Lord hosted a luncheon for the delegation.

After the most enjoyable lunch with Mrs. Lord, the delegation held a press conference with the domestic and foreign press. It was attended by over a hundred TV and newspaper journalists and provided us with an opportunity to build bridges through the media.

### *Xian and Quilin, August 19-21*

After the press conference, fourteen of the delegates went on to China's ancient capital, Xian, and the most scenic city in the country, Guilin. They toured Huaqing Hot Springs and the Xian Museum and wit-

Delegation with President Keging Kang, *fifth from L, first row,* and Vice-President Jiegiong Lei, *third from L, first row*. Photo courtesy of Dr. Lily K. Lai.

Delegation met with Ambassador Winston Lord and Mrs. Bette Bao Lord, *fifth and sixth from the R, second row*, at the U.S. Embassy. Photo courtesy of Dr. Lily K. Lai.

Delegation at press conference in Beijing. Photo courtesy of Dr. Lily K. Lai.

nessed the fabulous display of the Qin terra-cotta soldier and horse figures. Then they flew to Guilin and unwound amidst the natural beauty of the city's mountains, rivers, and caverns. To their surprise, the deputy mayor of Guilin, Fenglian Yuan, hosted a delicious dinner in their honor during their last evening in China. An architect by profession, Yuan told the delegates her ambitious modernization plans of building more roads, bridges, and hotels in the beautiful city of Guilin.

## Summary of Official Discussions in China

China was obviously in transition. As mentioned earlier, there were two different forms of Chinese currency: foreign currency certificates for foreign visitors and people money for Chinese people. There were big state-owned enterprises and small private companies. There were China Friendship Stores just for foreign visitors and regular stores for everyone.

President Chen of the People's Bank of China told us that women in China had made tremendous progress. For example, about 40 percent of the workers in the financial field were women. There were many outstanding women in key positions in politics, economics, technology, culture, and education. In addition to President Chen, other high-ranking women in finance included the vice-chair of the People's Bank of China, the president of the Bank of Industry and Commerce, and two other women vice-presidents who specialized in finance for agriculture and transportation, respectively. Women leaders in industry-related positions included the minister of textile industry and the minister of water resources and electric power. The latter had supervised the taming of the Yellow River, which had historically caused massive flooding damages in China.

The delegates learned from President Kang that the two most urgent problems facing China were controlling the population growth and combating illiteracy. According to President Kang, it was necessary to control China's population growth because China had one-quarter of the world's population but only occupied 7 percent of the world's arable land. There were 300 million children between the ages of 0 to 14 among more than fifty-six ethnic groups in China. This presented a major problem for policy makers. China had just implemented a compulsory education program aimed at eliminating illiteracy, which was prevalent in China. Although China had made significant progress in economic reform, it must intensify the education of its people in order for the economic development to continue.

Ambassador Lord stated, "China is a friend, but not an ally, not like Japan and the NATO [North Atlantic Treaty Organization] allies." There was isolation and hostility between the United States and China for almost three decades. President Nixon and four other U.S. presidents following him and many other people had continuously worked to strengthen bilateral relations, while maintaining friendship with Taiwan. Also, in the area of national security, America and China had different views on Vietnam, Afghanistan, and North and South Korea. Although China had been improving its relationship with the Soviet Union, it still welcomed an American presence in Asia since it believed that this helped to stabilize the region. Ambassador Lord said that U.S. trade with China had been slow and difficult. This had been due to the lack of a legal structure for business in general and contracts in particular, restrictions on access to the Chinese domestic markets by foreign companies, a shortage of hard currency, and a lack of understanding of Chinese culture among American businesspeople. While optimistic about the potential for developing trade opportunities with China, Ambassador Lord stressed that Americans must learn to be patient and understand that "trade is a two-way street." China must be able to sell in America before it could buy from Americans. With regard to the U.S. position on China and Taiwan, Ambassador Lord was very clear that the people on both sides of the

Taiwan Straits must solve the problem between China and Taiwan by themselves.

Mrs. Lord, an accomplished writer and a Chinese American woman leader herself, believed that Chinese American women would be a perfect bridge to bring together the two diverse cultures. This could serve to promote better understanding and friendship between the two countries. Mrs. Lord shared with us that she was heading a project to help Chinese performing groups modify their presentations to make them more acceptable to international audiences. Mrs. Lord said that Chinese performers had a very high degree of skills, but because they were not attuned to presenting themselves to a foreign audience, they did not receive the attention they deserved. Thus her purpose was to work with them to improve their presentations so that Chinese culture could be shared and appreciated by a much broader audience.

## Personal Reflections of a Delegate

As the national president of OCAW, I was honored to cochair this important delegation with the Honorable Anna Chennault. I would like to thank Pauline W. Tsui, Margot Wei, Faith Breen, and many other people who worked tirelessly to make this visit a success. I would also like to thank AT&T and US West International for their financial support for the trip.

We were warmly welcomed and had productive meetings everywhere we went in Taiwan, China, and Hong Kong. It was obvious to us that they were at different stages of social, economic, educational, and political development. However, we met outstanding women leaders and had happy memories in all the cities we visited.

I have traveled to Taiwan, Hong Kong, and China at least three or four times a year for at least fifteen years following this 1987 OCAW trip, and I could see the rapid changes every time I visited the same places. Most changes were good, but I was very sorry that the Taiwanese government abolished the uniform college entrance examination system because the system provided fair and equitable opportunities for many good students from disadvantaged families. I was one of the beneficiaries of such a system.

The delegates met many accomplished and inspiring women leaders during the trip, and some of them became friends of OCAW and personal friends of some of the delegates, including myself.

The delegation was the first Chinese American group going from

> the United States to Taiwan and then to Hong Kong and China in one trip. This ice-breaking trip, in our professional estimation, produced an unexpected result: it planted the seed for the open-door policy between Taiwan and China and hastened the agreement of the two governments to allow people on both sides of the Taiwan Straits to visit each other.

So ends Dr. Lily K. Lai's detailed and informative report on OCAW's August 1987 Women-to-Women Exchange Program.

## OCAW Continues to Network in the 1980s

During November 20–22, 1987, the Los Angeles Chapter hosted OCAW's Tenth Anniversary National Conference at the Los Angeles Sheraton Universal Hotel, with over one hundred participants. The conference theme was "Chinese American Women Today and Tomorrow." Conference workshops focused on the following three themes:

1. Strengthening Ourselves
2. Strengthening Our Careers
3. Strengthening Our Families

The keynote speaker was the Honorable Mae Yeh, state senator of Oregon. Her topic was "The Making of a Politician," in which she made four points: (1) How I became involved in the political process; (2) how to run for political office; (3) how to stay in office; and (4) why we should run for political office.

Ms. Yeh strongly stated, "We have to be part of the decision making process to control our own destiny. We need to have Chinese Americans, preferably women, elected at the national level so that we will have a voice to represent the Chinese Americans' interests and concerns."

Pauline Lo Alker, president and CEO of Counterpoint Computer, Inc., was the other keynote speaker, and she discussed how she became involved in politics and encouraged us to do likewise.

An award banquet was held honoring Julia Chang Bloch, assistant administrator, Bureau for Asia and Near East, U.S. AID; Betty Tom Chu, chairman and CEO, Trust Savings Bank; and Beulah Quo, actress and cofounder and first vice-president of the Association of Asian Pacific American Artists. Frances Wu, Ph.D., received a special achievement award for her work with the Chinese American Golden Age Association.

The conference chair was Cecilia Yu, and banquet chairs were OCAW Los Angeles Chapter president Linda Lum and Chapter president-elect, Lois Lee.

During January 6–8, 1988, OCAW joined forces with the National Federation of Business and Professional Women's organizations in participating in the Women's Agenda II Conference in Kansas City, Missouri. Faith Lee Breen, Ph.D., on behalf of OCAW, served as the temporary conference chair at its final plenary session.

During 1989–1991, OCAW actively supported the formation of the Association of Professional Asian American Women, the Filipina American Women's Network, and the Asian American Voters Coalition. All these organizations presented OCAW's executive director with an award of appreciation.

On December 8, 1989, the students of Peace and Human Rights at the American University, Washington, D.C., presented Pauline W. Tsui with an award for Outstanding Contributions to the Realization of Human Rights in the Metropolitan Washington, D.C., Area for her work with OCAW.

On November 1, 1988, OCAW coordinated with over forty organizations in hosting a dinner honoring the Honorable Elaine L. Chao, chairperson of the U.S. Federal Maritime Commission, and the Honorable Wendy Lee Gramm, chairperson of the U.S. Commodity Future Trading Commission. The dinner was held at Tony Cheng's Seafood Restaurant, Washington, D.C. These were the highest federal positions to which Asian American women were ever appointed.

On September 8, 1989, OCAW, with fifteen other Asian American organizations, celebrated the appointment of the first Asian American ambassador, a woman, the Honorable Julia Chang Bloch, to the Kingdom of Nepal. This latest presidential appointment capped a distinguished, trailblazing career in the public sector as an Asian American woman. The grand reception was held at the Botanical Garden, Washington, D.C.

On September 12, 1989, OCAW hosted a lunch for Taiwan's women leaders who were mostly journalists, at the University Club, Washington, D.C. The delegation was exceedingly impressed by the guest speaker, Michael Weisskoff of the *Washington Post,* a China expert, who had just returned from a trip to China.

OCAW's Sixth Biennial National Conference took place at the J.W. Marriott Hotel in Washington, D.C. October 26–29, 1989. The theme was "Chinese American Women: Preparing for the 21st Century." An awards banquet was held on Thursday, October 26, and the White House briefing was held on Friday, October 27. The topic of the White House

OCAW 1989 National Conference, Washington, D.C., *L to R:* Anita Wong, Hawai'i Chapter member, and Faith Lee Breen, Ph. D., 1989 OCAW national chair.

briefing was "International Business and Trades: Breaking the Trade Barrier and Creating New Opportunities in Pacific Rim Countries."

The Honorable Elaine L. Chao, deputy secretary-designate, U.S. Department of Transportation, was the keynote speaker on Saturday, October 27, and Linda Yu, ABC anchor for Chicago, was the luncheon speaker that day.

Workshops were offered on the following topics:

1. 200 Years in Hawaii: Moving Forward in America
2. What It Takes to get Ahead
3. Managing Your Career Change
4. U.S./China Trade
5. International Business and Trade Opportunities in the Global Economy
6. Owning, Operating and Developing a Small Business
7. Establishing Your Leadership Style
8. Getting Contracts from the Federal Government
9. PASS (Procurement, Automated Source System)
10. Strategies for Success
11. Power Politics
12. Our Leadership Style

In 1989, OCAW and the U.S. Pan Asian American Chamber of Commerce (USPAACC) collaborated to sponsor the first of several Excellence 2000 Awards Banquets. This program was to recognize the special achievements of Asian Americans in education, arts, science, sports, business, civic and public service. At the time of its first public program, it was the only collective and cooperative effort with the Asian community that brought together the diverse cultures and interests of the broader Asian American community.

The theme of that evening's Excellence 2000 Awards Program, was "Celebrating a Decade of Excellence in Youth, Education, Arts, Science, and Business." Master of Ceremonies was Congressman Norman Y. Mineta. Sixteen honorees were the following:

1. Hon. Julia Chang Bloch, U.S. ambassador to Kingdom of Nepal
2. Hon. Elaine L. Chao, deputy secretary, U.S. Department of Transportation
3. Hon. Anna Claire Chennault, president, TAC International, Inc.
4. Lilia A. Clemente, chairperson, Clemente Capital, Inc.
5. David Henry Hwang, Tony Award–winning playwright
6. Yong C. Kim, chairman, CEO Y.Y.K. Enterprises, Inc.
7. Haesun Paik, winner, William Kapell International Piano Competition
8. Dith Pran, *New York Times* photojournalist
9. Theodore, W.J. Wong, president, Missile Systems Group, Hughes Aircraft Co.
10. John T.C. Yeh, president, Integrated Microcomputer Systems, Inc.
11. – 16. Westinghouse Science Talent Search Contest finalists: Divya Chandler, Vijay Pande, Janet Tseng, Albert Wong, Weina Yu Sieh, and Wei-jing Zhu

Conference sponsors were the National OCAW and the OCAW Chesapeake Chapter. The conference chair was Pauline W. Tsui. Linda Chen, OCAW Chesapeake Chapter president, was the conference cochair. The award banquet cochairs were Lily K. Lai, Ph.D., OCAW national president, and Susan Au Allen, J.D., president, USPAACC and OCAW national vice-president.

In the evening of November 20, 1989, OCAW presented a vocal gala at the John F. Kennedy Center for the Performing Arts, Washington, D.C., to raise funds for music scholarships. Performing artists were Cecilia Min Tsai, soprano from Taiwan, Mau Hua Zhan, mezzo-soprano from Shanghai, Liu Qiang Zu, tenor from Beijing, Sun Yu, bass-baritone from Beijing, and

Andres Maspero, pianist. The producer-director of this program was Muriel Hom, teacher of piano and a voice coach.

At the request of Senators Tom Daschle and Paul Simon, two OCAW members testified before a U.S. Senate panel in November 1988 on behalf of OCAW on the following issues:

1. "College Admission Policy Should be Based Upon Individual Merit," by Faith Lee Breen, Ph.D., associate professor of business and management and economics
2. "Support an Immigration Policy That Reflects the Family Values of All Americans Which Include the Reunification of the Nuclear Family and Economic Growth through Competitiveness" by Susan Au Allen, J.D.

Pauline W. Tsui, executive director of OCAW, requested of Daschle and Simon that the above two testimonies be included in the *Congressional Record.*

To identify strategic opportunities essential to achieving success for the future of the organization, OCAW held its first training sessions for its board on January 14, 1989, entitled "Essentials of Successful Board and Training Workshop." The trainer was Mary Gonzalez Wiersma. The training topics that composed the agenda were as follows:

1. Introductions and Expectations
2. Objectives
3. Accomplishments
4. Values
5. Mission
6. Where Do We Want to Be in Five Years?
7. Goals for 1989

CHAPTER 3

# EXPANDING OUR REACH

## THE 1990s

The second Excellence 2000 Award Banquet, sponsored by OCAW and U.S. Pan Asian American Chamber of Commerce, was held on September 27, 1990, at the Hyatt Regency Hotel, Washington, D.C. The theme was "Proud to be American." Presentation of colors was by the Armed Forces Color Guard, and the Pledge of Allegiance was led by John T. C. Yeh.

The sixteen awardees were as follows:

1. Amar G. Bose, Ph.D., chairman and CEO of Bose Corporation
2. Rear Admiral Ming E. Chang, U.S. Navy
3. Jorge Garcia, M.D., chief, cardiac surgery, Washington Hospital Center
4. Raymond K.K. Ho, president and CEO, Maryland Public TV
5. Narayan Keshavan, special Washington correspondent to *New York City Tribune*
6. Harry Lee, J.D., sheriff, Jefferson Parish Sheriff Office, Metairie, Louisiana
7. Sammy Lee, M.D., two-time U.S. Olympic national gold medalist in high platform diving; bronze medalist; inducted into the U.S. Olympic Hall of Fame in 1990
8. Haing S. Ngor, M.D., television and film actor, author, and medical doctor
9. Pauline W. Tsui, cofounder and executive director, OCAW; president, D.C. Chinatown Service Center; chair of D.C. Commission on Asian and Pacific Affairs, 1988
10. Tswen-Ling Tsui (posthumously), executive director, National Chinese Welfare Council; executive secretary, Sino-American Cultural Society; advisor, Chinese Consolidated Benevolent Association; consultant to Coordination Council for North American Affairs; presi-

dent, General Business Investment Corp; legislative assistant to former senator Hiram L. Fong of Hawai'i

11. Grant Ujifusa, coauthor and founding editor, *Almanac of American Politics;* senior editor, *Reader's Digest;* legislative strategy chair, Japanese American Citizen's League Redress Effort
12. Kristi Yamaguchi, U.S. Olympic national gold medalist in ice skating in pairs and silver medalist in ladies singles
13. – 16. The four Youth and Education awardees were David Liu, Royce Y. Peng, Soojin Ryu, and Mina Kim Yu

Remarks were given by Hon. Elaine L. Chao, deputy secretary of the U.S. Department of Transportation. The keynote speaker was Hon. David S.C. Chu, Ph.D., assistant secretary, U.S. Department of Defense. Carole A. Presley, Ph.D., senior vice-president, Federal Express Corporation, was a guest speaker.

The banquet chair was Susan Au Allen, Esq., president, USPAACC, and national vice-president OCAW. The banquet vice-chairs were Faith Lee Breen, Ph.D., chair of OCAW National Board, president and owner of System Resource Management Inc. and associate professor, Prince George's Community College, and William H. Marumoto, founder and chairman of the board of Interface Group, Ltd.

The 1990 Combined Federal Campaign approved OCAW's application for participation to receive funds in the national capital area.

On June 1–2, 1991, OCAW held its second Strategic Planning Session for its board at the IBM Corporation Conference room, Washington, D.C. The aim was to "facilitate the formulation of an action plan to capitalize on identified strategic opportunities." The trainer was Nancy Linn Patton, OCAW national president, 1991–1993. Sixteen strengths and twenty weaknesses of OCAW were identified and discussed. Patton discussed the following major issues with the group:

1. Mission and Goals Identification
2. Financial Plans and Sources
3. Organizational Structure
4. Membership
5. Communications and Public Relations
6. Program Development

In 1993, OCAW initiated a survey for the Chinese American Retirement Enterprise, Inc., and published a report titled "1993 Survey of

Needs for Low-Income Elderly Housing," in Metropolitan Washington, D.C. OCAW actively supported this project in building an eighty-nine-unit apartment complex to help meet the urgent needs of our elderly population.

## OPERA INTERNATIONAL BY LINDA DEVINE

OCAW is proud to have supported the initiation and ongoing program of Opera International, founded by Muriel Hom. It started with four vocal concerts from 1989 to 1993 and blossomed into the production of eleven operas from 1994 to 2004 and five operatic concerts from 2005 to 2009. We asked Linda Devine, editor of OCAW's e-newsletter and daughter of Muriel, to write about Opera International. Linda's story follows, based on her interview of her mother and further research.

> Created out of a love for opera and its artists, Opera International is a company founded by Muriel Hom in 1994 under the auspices of OCAW. It has been very successful over the years, richly fulfilling its threefold mission of (1) encouraging and inspiring in young people an appreciation of opera; (2) training and preparing aspiring vocalists of all nationalities for operatic careers; and (3) offering world-class opera at affordable prices.
>
> Hom and her brother and sister, orphaned at an early age, were raised by their grandmother in quarters above King's Restaurant, a popular Chinese eating establishment in Washington, D.C., that was the family business. She and her siblings worked hard at the restaurant from the time they were young. Muriel was nine years old when family friend Esther Wy came over to Muriel's home and played "I'm in the Mood for Love" on the piano. It made a deep impression upon her, and she thought to herself, "I would love to play the piano like that."
>
> Muriel started taking piano lessons and was a child prodigy by age ten. Her talent was so noteworthy that she was featured in an article in the *Washington Herald*, one of the major Washington newspapers of the time. Although traveling at a young age precluded her participation, she was even invited to perform in New York City on the prestigious *Major Bowes Amateur Hour*, America's best-known talent show of the time, broadcast by the CBS Radio Network.

Muriel Hom, affectionately known as Mimi, founder and producer-director of Opera International. Photo courtesy of Linda Devine.

Her piano teacher took her to her first opera performance, Mozart's *Cosi Fan Tutte,* when Muriel was eleven. She enjoyed it so much that it was a turning point for her, and she was to have a lifelong career in music. Fast-forward to the 90s.

Hom was honored in Taiwan in 1991 and by OCAW in 1995 for her long-standing dedication to aiding, developing, and promoting singers. She has been the vice-president for programs of OCAW for over twenty years, and she currently is president of the D.C. Federation of Music Clubs as well as director of music at the Hermon Presbyterian Church in Bethesda, Maryland.

While working with singers, Hom noticed that many international performers were being critically acclaimed and receiving worldwide attention, but this was not occurring with Chinese artists. She knew that they were very talented, but they were not receiving the recognition she felt they deserved, so she decided to create a platform for them. She approached Pauline W. Tsui, then OCAW's executive director, and proposed that OCAW sponsor a concert to present these singers at the renowned John F. Kennedy Center for the Performing Arts in Washington, D.C. Tsui liked the idea and gave Hom the approval to go ahead.

On November 20, 1989, the first concert was presented in the Terrace Theater of the Kennedy Center. It was billed as the "Vocal Gala," featuring Cecilia Min Tsai, soprano; Man Hua Zhan, mezzo-soprano; Lin Qiang Xu, tenor; and Sun Yu, bass-baritone, all accompanied by pianist Andres Maspero. The concert was very well received, as evidenced by positive reviews in the *Washington Post*.

In April 1991, Hom presented the second successful Kennedy Center concert, this time featuring tenor Jianyi Zhang and violinist Qian Zhou. At this point, enter the Li Foundation, which was to have the single most positive effect on Opera International, with its enduring financial support. The Li Foundation was founded in 1944 by the late Dr. Kuo Ching Li and his four brothers to promote friendly relations between the United States and China through educational and scholarly exchange. Dr. Li was the founder of the Wah Chang Corporation, originally an international tungsten ore and concentrate trading company in New York. The work of the foundation has been carried on by Dr. Li's children and grandchildren, and over the years it has provided numerous fellowships in the United States to promising students and scholars from China.

For this concert, Hom invited a friend, Dr. Edward Leong Way of

San Francisco, California, to attend. She wanted to show him what actions she was taking to advance Chinese singers. At the time, Dr. Way was president of the Li Foundation and was also the husband of Hom's best friend, Madeline Li Leong Way, chief executive officer of the foundation. Dr. Way was very impressed with the high level of the entire performance, and thus began the Li Foundation's association with OCAW. Since 1991, the foundation has provided generous grants to the organization as part of the foundation's fellowship program for upcoming, talented artists. Mezzo-soprano Zheng Cao and soprano Haibo Bai were the first OCAW recipients of Li Foundation scholarships.

In November 1992, a third Kennedy Center concert, another "Vocal Gala," was held in honor of the Li Foundation in appreciation of its generous support. Soprano Guiping Deng, Zheng Cao, and Sun Yu performed.

In November 1993, a fourth and final concert delighted audiences. The event featured young, internationally acclaimed cellist

Kennedy Center Concert: On November 1, 1992, the Li Foundation was honored at a Vocal Gala Benefit Concert produced and directed by Mimi Hom at the Kennedy Center Terrace Theater under the auspices of OCAW.

Hai-ye Ni, whose career was steeply on the rise and who went on to perform with the New York Philharmonic and Philadelphia Orchestras. She is considered one of the great cellists of her generation. Hai-bo Bai also was featured, and Sun Yu sang once again. Bai and Yu performed duets from two of Mozart's operas, and renowned *Washington Post* critic Joseph McLellan wrote, "I have seen these duets performed countless times in some of the world's leading opera houses, but I cannot remember seeing them done with better voices or better awareness of style and dynamics."

In December 1993, Hom approached conductor Edward Roberts and stage director Muriel Von Villas and asked them if they would join her in producing *The Marriage of Figaro (Le nozze di Figaro).* They agreed to the project.

For Opera International's opera, "international" was indeed an accurate descriptor, as its cast featured singers from the United States, China, Taiwan, Korea, Puerto Rico, and Brazil. The major roles were performed by Ding Gao (Figaro), Myra Merritt (Susanna), Adriana Moura (Cherubino), Sun Yu (Count Almaviva), and Hai-bo Bai (Countess Almaviva). Hom was producer-director, Roberts served as conductor and music director, and Von Villas was artistic and stage director. With a modest budget of $55,000 for the entire production, the sets were elegant but simple and costumes were whatever could be obtained from the closets of the performers, augmented by items such as numerous inexpensive skirts and shoes purchased from K-Mart and Payless Shoe Source by Director of Operations Gaylyn Mercer.

Opera International's first opera, *The Marriage of Figaro,* was presented on August 14, 1994, at the Lisner Auditorium of George Washington University in Washington, D.C. The production was a great success, as evidenced by a glowing review in the *Washington Post* by critic Joseph McLellan, who titled his article "A World-Class Debut" and summed up the production as a "dazzling performance." *Intermission* magazine called the opera "dashing.... Producer-director Muriel Hom brings years of musical mastery and a teacher's loving dedication to this company. They were well-served by her in this production."

With the production's resounding success, Hom was encouraged to continue. Thus, Opera International was firmly established in 1994 as a continuing company under the auspices of OCAW.

In August 1995, Opera International presented its second opera, Mozart's *Cosi Fan Tutte.* Costume designer Charles Caine and make-up and wig designer James Geier joined the production staff and remained with Opera International throughout the company's subsequent years.

The *Washington Post* called the production "a first-class '*Cosi Fan Tutte.*'" It praised the singers, saying they "all...were excellent vocally and theatrically," and "not only in individual performances, but especially in the crucial ensembles." Also applauded were the "skilled conducting" by Roberts and the "deft, witty, finely detailed stage direction" of Von Villas.

After *Figaro* and *Cosi,* audience members commented that it was unfortunate that such great productions were seen only one time. It was then decided to expand the company's scope and stage two performances per year—a Friday evening gala and a Sunday matinee performance.

This was put in motion for Opera International's third opera in 1996, Puccini's *La Boheme.* The cast and sets were expanded to accommodate the requirements for this opera at a budget of $125,000—over double that of *Figaro.*

The opera required a large chorus and children's chorus. In addition, many supernumeraries were needed, and these individuals were thrilled to fill small, non singing, acting roles such as waiters and band members.

The production was a huge success. "Well-Crafted '*La Boheme,*'" headlined McLellan's review for the *Washington Post*. The *Review* (Washington, D.C.) praised that "this company of singers offered a fresh, youthful approach to the 100-year-old opera."

In 1997, Puccini's *Madame Butterfly (Madama Butterfly)* was the fourth opera selected. The two-performance experiment of the previous year had worked well, so again, Friday evening and Sunday afternoon events were planned. Among the principals in the cast were Hai-bo Bai, Zheng Cao, Sun Yu, and Chen-ye Yuan, all recipients of Li Foundation scholarships, demonstrating the role that the foundation played in the development of young, promising artists. These singers and other Li Foundation scholarship recipients have all gone on to illustrious careers. They have sung opera internationally and have been invited to conduct master classes overseas. *Butterfly* received excellent reviews in the *Washington Post*, as well as in the *Review* and *Intermission*.

Opera International's influence on children has been significant. In addition to young people attending the productions with their parents and being exposed to fine classical music at an early age, oth-

Scene from *Madame Butterfly,* a 1997 production of Opera International. Photo courtesy of Linda Devine.

ers were given opportunities to be involved in the productions themselves. In *La Boheme,* two dozen youngsters were given the chance to sing in the children's chorus. Zachary Roberts was among them, and he sang in other company productions as well. In *Madame Butterfly,* young Jennifer Olsen-Simpson played the small part of Butterfly's child, Little Sorrow. Also in *Butterfly,* seven-year-old Amanda Devine and Stephanie Hom performed as young geishas in supernumerary roles. The girls learned the discipline and patience of attending long rehearsals lasting way past their normal bedtimes, but they were thrilled with the opportunity to be a part of the magnificent production. They have enduring memories as a result.

Throughout the years, many volunteers have contributed to Opera International's success. June Tong has served in the important role of administrative director from the outset, Hong-fa Chu took over as director of operations. Trudy Grant has lent much support as director of communications. These individuals in particular have been called upon to perform a wide variety of duties and their tremendous efforts have been critical to the success of the company.

In 1998, Rossini's *The Barber of Seville (Il Barbiere di Siviglia)* was Opera International's fifth production. The cast was again international, with members hailing from the United States, China, Korea, Austria, and Peru. The *Washington Post* described the performance of the classic, comic opera as "smooth, musically polished, and beautifully coordinated," highlighting its "cutting humor."

In 1999, Opera International presented its sixth opera, Puccini's powerful, dramatic *Tosca.* Along with a cast from the United States, China, Taiwan, and Peru, *Tosca* also featured a boys' chorus, and once again Opera International's positive influence on children was highlighted. Classmates Kevin Huang, Michael Sidgmore, Jed Bergman, and William Snyderwine joined others to constitute the chorus, and they were delighted with the opportunity to be a part of the production. These ten- and eleven-year-old boys were competitive athletes, and opera was not something they really had been exposed to before. Hom trained them for their roles. The Italian lyrics were difficult for them, and the music was very intricate, but after a month they had learned their parts well. Von Villas then directed them on how to act. With much practice and dedication, they performed beautifully. This unique event opened up a whole new world to them. In the end, Kevin and Michael enjoyed their experience so much that they donated their honorarium checks back to Opera International, and the four families have been financial contributors to the company since then.

The production also provided another opportunity for a rising young singer, demonstrating once again that Opera International's interest in young artists extended to children. Boy soprano Zachary Eden Bernhard performed in the role of the shepherd boy. Subsequently, Zachary went on to New York to sing the same role with the Metropolitan Opera. *Tosca* received superb reviews in the *Washington Post*, the *Gazette* (Maryland), and the *Review*.

Opera International's seventh and eighth operas in 2000, combined in one production, were two smaller one-act operas by Puccini, *Il Tabarro* and *Gianni Schicchi,* with a cast hailing from China, Korea, Mexico, and the United States. The *Gazette* described the performances as "two gems from Opera International." The singing and acting in the dramatic, dark *Il Tabarro* were cited as "masterful" and "pure passion." By contrast, the lighthearted *Gianni Schicchi* was "delightful." For both operas, "the singers gave us the excellence we have come to expect" from Opera International.

Verdi's *Falstaff,* Opera International's ninth opera, followed in

2001. Seven elementary school–aged children performed supernumerary roles as elves and fairies. Among them was eight-year-old Tommy Devine, who enjoyed the uplifting music so much that to this day, as a college student, he often studies classical music. *Falstaff* received enthusiastic reviews.

In 2002, Opera International presented its tenth opera, Francesco Cavalli's *L'Ormindo,* a baroque opera. To reflect the earlier time period, some different instruments were added to the small orchestra—among them the harpsichord, baroque guitar, lute, theorbo, and flue organ. Although this work was a departure from the company's previous norm, the opera was yet again given positive reviews by the *Washington Post*, which summed it up as "a rare treat."

To celebrate the tenth season of Opera International, a Tenth Season Opera Gala was held in 2003, featuring selected acts from *The Marriage of Figaro* as well as Verdi's *Otello* and *Rigoletto.* Fourteen superb artists participated in the gala, including internationally acclaimed Wei Song, director of the Opera Troupe of the Shanghai Opera House.

Its eleventh opera was presented in 2004. It was Francis Poulenc's *Dialogues of the Carmelites.* Performers were from the United States, China, Taiwan, Canada, and Puerto Rico, and the *Washington Post* review applauded both their vocal and dramatic abilities. As it was the tenth anniversary of Opera International's existence, the company hosted a joyous champagne reception following the Friday evening performance to celebrate the milestone. The excellent production came at a cost, though, with the $240,000 budget being Opera International's highest to date.

Hom's skillful fundraising efforts had yielded the funds required to stage these performances thus far, but it was becoming more and more difficult. So in 2005, Hom went in a different direction in that she produced a series of Operatic Vocal Gala Concerts, with her fifth in 2009.

Outstanding donors to which the company is particularly indebted are coproducer Mei-jong C. Hung, the Li Foundation, the Bureau of National Affairs, Inc., the Morris & Gwendolyn Cafritz Foundation, the Herman Lissner Foundation, and the Nancy Peery Marriott Foundation. Other significant contributors have been Pauline W. Tsui and the Dr. and Mrs. John Y. Woo Memorial Fund, the Han Wang Memorial Fund, the Ruth H. Kuo and Rhoda How Memorial Foundation, the Montgomery County Community Foundation, Dr. Adson I. Chuang, Muriel

Hom, Betty Jean Wen, David and Teresa Ma, Esther C. Wy, Janet and John Biermann, and Amy C. Lee. Opera International, however, has appreciated *all* gifts, both large and small. It is this spirit of generosity, as well as the pure enjoyment of beautiful music, that has united us all.

Hom said in an interview, "If you really want to convert people to opera, you have to present something good." Presenting something good, though, requires money. Throughout the years, in addition to contributions by generous donors—including Mei-jong Hung, who joined Hom as coproducer, Opera International has held fundraisers to support its productions. Hai-bo Bai and Hong-fu Chu are to be especially commended for arranging and singing in multiple benefit concerts over the years.

## Second Continental Congress for Women of the Americas Conference

On February 18, 1994, OCAW cosponsored the Second Continental Congress for Women of the Americas Conference. The conference theme was "Strength through Communication," and it was held in Washington, D.C. The conference cochairs were the Honorable Anna Chennault and Katherine Chang Dress.

The purpose for the conference was for women from North, South, and Central America to establish communication and learn from each other. Several hundred women from diverse geographical locations attended. Conference discussions were on the following topics:

1. Self-Empowerment and Equity
2. Education, Literacy, and Retraining
3. Arts, Sports, Culture
4. Family
5. Politics, Public Administration
6. Business, Economy, Employment
7. Environment
8. Health

## OCAW Continues to Reach Out

In 1994, OCAW launched a series of Power Lunches in Washington, D.C. the Honorable Linda Tsao Yang, U.S. executive director on the Board of Directors of the Asian Development Bank in Manila, was one of the first two honorees. She was the first woman executive director appointed by the U.S government to the board of a multilateral development bank. She was appointed by President Clinton and confirmed by the U.S. Senate. She was also the first minority and first woman appointed to serve as California's savings and loans commissioner from 1980 to 1982. Carol F. Lee, J.D., was the other honoree. She served as general counsel of the Export-Import Bank of the United States. She was a partner in the Washington, D.C., law firm of Wilmer, Cutter and Pickering from 1983 to 1993.

On June 12, 1994, OCAW welcomed back Ambassador Julia Chang Bloch at a dinner in Bethesda, Maryland. Cosponsors with OCAW of the dinner, were the Sino-American Cultural Society and OCA–D.C. Chapter. The title of the speech delivered by Ambassador Bloch was "Pacific Rim Economic and Trade Outlook and Experiences in the Kingdom of Nepal as U.S. Ambassador." She said that during the five years in Nepal, she witnessed the transformation of Nepal from a centuries-old monarchy to a fledgling democracy. Her job was to keep President Bush and the State Department informed of what was happening there and to determine what steps had to be taken to assure the safety of U.S. citizens in Nepal. Now, in her new position as group vice-president of the Bank of America, the objective of her unit was to provide the bank's customers in thirty-seven countries with a comprehensive variety of financial services and products. A good deal of that business is done in the Pacific Rim.

On May 14, 1995, OCAW began an annual Salute to Mothers Banquet. The purpose was to underscore the unrelenting drive with which Asian American women traditionally work to provide their children the best educational opportunities. This event was the brainchild of Christiana Chiang, who chaired its committee. The evening took place at the Hyatt Regency Hotel, Crystal City, Virginia, and the mistress of ceremony was Kaity Tong, anchor woman of WPIX–New York.

The after-dinner entertainment was a glittering fashion show produced by Grace Lee, featuring stunning formal Chinese gowns graciously loaned by Cynthia Hsu's Cindy's Bridal Inc. A series of preshow modeling training sessions given by Grace Lee, also pro bono, was invaluable to the young models.

On May 11, 1996, a Salute to Mothers and Award Banquet was held at the Hyatt Regency Hotel, Crystal City, Virginia, cosponsored by OCAW and the Washington Chinese Television. The honorees were Senator Paul B. Simon and his wife, Dr. Jean Simon, both of whom were awarded the OCAW Pillar Awards; Jeanie Jew, creator of the Asian Pacific American Heritage Month; Ruby Moy, who received the OCAW Leadership Award;

and Christiana Chiang, who received the OCAW Community Service Award.

The after-dinner fashion show, again produced by Grace Lee, featured clothes loaned by Limited and Cache, showing the fashions of the younger generations.

Also, in 1996, OCAW joined OCA and eighteen other organizations in encouraging the participation of Asian Pacific Americans in voter registration held on Capitol Hill. The group emphasized voter's education and stressed the importance of making Asian Pacific Americans voices heard.

A successful outcome of OCAW's English classes in Washington's Chinatown was the opening of a hair design saloon in Montgomery County, Maryland, by a student in 1993. She was a new immigrant who learned enough English from OCAW's classes—taught by Katherine Chang Dress—to become an owner of the business of her dreams.

OCAW received an extremely appreciated grant from the Herman Lissner Foundation in 1997 through the gracious assistance of Teresa and David Ma. The grant enabled OCAW to rent a national office in Bethesda, Maryland, a suburb of Washington, D.C., where parking was next door and a subway station only half a block away. On January 11, 1997, OCAW held an Open House Reception in its grand office space.

The easy accessibility of the office enabled OCAW to offer a series of continuing career advancement training classes for its 1981 nonprofessional training graduates. These courses on basic computer use were conducted pro bono by Cathy C. Roberts twice a week for five weeks in each course. Within a year, we witnessed the positive effects these classes had on the lives of the students.

One graduate switched her job from a Chinese restaurant to a bank teller and was later promoted to a supervisory position in no time. The transformation of OCAW's training in nonprofessional students' lives was indeed phenomenal.

The multiyear funding from the Herman Lissner Foundation enabled OCAW not only to maintain the national office but also to fund Opera International and Presidential Classroom scholarships, plus a seminary student's scholarship.

## OCAW's Twentieth Anniversary National Conference

Held April 25–27, 1997, the conference theme was "Twenty Years of Leadership and Service to the Community." On Friday, April 25, a White House

January 11, 1997, OCAW Open House at new national headquarters, 4641 Montgomery Avenue, Suite 208, Bethesda, Maryland. OCAW members attending, *front row, L to R:* Minerva Eng, Margarette Yu Goldstein, Rose Li, Pauline W. Tsui, Christiana Chiang, Anni Dan; *back row, L to R:* Jeanie F.L. Jew, Cecilia Ouspensky, Henriette Levy, Christine Lee, Kathy Dress, Grace Lee, June Tang Williamson, Christina Wong. Photo courtesy of Jeanie F.L. Jew.

tour and briefing were conducted. On Saturday, April 26, the conference and workshops were held at the Rayburn House Office Building of the United States in Washington, D.C. Both events were sponsored by Congresswoman Constance A. Morella, with assistance from her legislative assistant, Mr. Ben Wu. On Sunday, April 27, at the Hyatt Regency Hotel, Crystal City, Virginia, a General OCAW Membership Meeting and Conference Summary was held, and in the evening, a "1997 Gala Banquet and Salute to Mothers" program was held, cosponsored by OCAW and Fraternidad Urkupina "Comite Pro-Bolivia."

Keynote speaker was Congresswoman Patsy T. Mink, who chaired

1997 OCAW Twentieth Anniversary National Conference, "Twenty Years of Leadership and Service to the Community," gathering of all eight OCAW national leaders from 1977 through 1997. *L to R:* Pauline W. Tsui, Ambassador Julia Chang Bloch, Hon. Lily Lee Chen, Lily K. Lai, Ph.D., Faith Lee Breen, Ph.D., Hon. Nancy Linn Patton, Hon. Katherine Chang Dress, and Jeanie F.L. Jew. Refer to appendix for years of leadership.

the Congressional Asian Pacific Caucus. Mink congratulated OCAW for its interests and programs that benefited Asian Pacific American women, as well as all women.

The workshops, held on Saturday, covered the following topics:

- Financial Independence through Entrepreneurship
- Managing Career Success
- Business and Government
- Know Your Rights: Legal Rights of Women/Domestic Violence
- Care For Your Health: Hormone Replacement Therapy and Menopause

The conference chair was Ms. Minerva Teng Eng.

The programs for the banquet included a fashion show entitled "The

Next Generation," produced by Grace Lee and Cynthia Hsu Jarboe, and several colorful Bolivian dances presented by Dora Castellon.

Presentation of OCAW awards was another highlight of the evening program: Ambassador Julia Chang Bloch and Stuart M. Bloch, Esq., received the Pillar Awards; the Honorable Katherine Chang Dress and Dr. Yeni Wong received the Leadership Awards; and the Community Service Award was presented to Dr. Jeffrey Fong.

In 1997 Jeanie F. Jew was elected national OCAW president, and in that capacity she was appointed to the new Gates Millennium Scholarship Program Advisory Committee, which enabled OCAW to assist minority students in applying for college financial aid.

Robert and Jeanie F.L. Jew, OCAW national president 1997–2001. Photo courtesy of Jeanie F.L. Jew.

## OCAW AND THE EDUCATION AND SCIENCE SOCIETY: DR. LUNGCHING CHIAO

We asked Lungching Chiao, Ed.D., vice-chairperson of the Education and Science Society (ESS), to write about OCAW's partnering with ESS since 1997. She and Molly Yen, manager of the Financial Aid to Rural Students Program/ESS, have taken numerous trips to China to visit and evaluate program sites. We congratulate ESS for its success in educational and social outreach programs in rural China. OCAW's coordinator for the Rural Scholarships Program was Pauline W. Tsui, who also served as translator of documents from Chinese to English upon donor requests, assisted by Ru Fan. Dr. Chiao added the following information about ESS and its outreach:

> Education and Science Society (ESS) is a nonprofit, nonpolitical educational organization, registered as a 501(c) (3) charitable organization in the state of New York. Its missions are to (1) promote understanding

**Table 1**
Geographical distribution of OCAW scholarship awards (1998–2011)

| PROVINCE/MUNICIPALITY | 1998 | 1999 | 2000 | 2001 | 2002 | 2003 | 2004 | 2005 | 2006 | 2007 | 2008 | 2009 | 2010 | 2011 | TOTAL |
|---|---|---|---|---|---|---|---|---|---|---|---|---|---|---|---|
| Chongqing 亘 | 9 | 9 | 9 | 11 | | | | | | | | | | | 38 |
| Gansu 甘 | 10 | 10 | 10 | | 19 | 19 | 8 | 8 | 8 | 39 | 29 | 24 | | | 184 |
| Guangxi 广西 | | 13 | 13 | | | | | | | | | | | | 26 |
| Guizhou 州 | | 12 | 12 | | | | | | | | | | | | 24 |
| Heilongjiang 江 | | | | | | | | | 9 | 9 | 11 | 5 | | | 34 |
| Henan 河南 | | | | 10 | 10 | 10 | | | | | | | | | 30 |
| Hunan 湖南 | | | | | | | 8 | 3 | 3 | | | | | | 14 |
| Liaoning 宁 | | | | | | | | 5 | 5 | 5 | | | | | 15 |
| NeiMenggu 内蒙 | | | 14 | | 12 | 12 | 11 | 8 | 16 | 19 | 11 | 4 | | | 107 |
| Ningxia 宁夏 | | | | | | | | 10 | 10 | 10 | | | | | 30 |
| Qinghai 海 | | 8 | 8 | 12 | 12 | 12 | | | | | | | | | 52 |
| Sichuan 四川 | 9 | 9 | 9 | | | | | | | | | 2 | | | 29 |
| Tibet 西藏 | | | | 10 | 10 | 10 | | 9 | 8 | 7 | | | | | 54 |
| Xingjiang 新疆 | | | | | 5 | 4 | | 4 | 4 | 4 | | | | | 21 |
| Yunnan 云南 | | 9 | 9 | 16 | 17 | 17 | | | | | | | 30 | 30 | 128 |
| Total | 28 | 70 | 84 | 59 | 85 | 84 | 27 | 47 | 63 | 93 | 51 | 35 | 30 | 30 | 786 |

Fourteen girls from Gansu Province, Tung Wei Prefecture, Shih Chuan Middle School, China (2009). Ms. Tung-hung Chen, ninth grade, *third from left, first row,* was one of 800 OCAW Scholarship recipients in the Education and Science Society, Inc. (ESS), Support Education in Rural China (SERC) Program. Photo courtesy of Molly Yen and Lungching Chiao, Ed.D., ESS.

between the peoples of the United States and China and (2) provide human and social development in rural China by raising literacy levels and improving the quality of education.

Providing Financial Aid for Rural Students (FARS) is one of the three major programs of Support Education in Rural China (SERC), a program series sponsored by ESS. Between 1997 and 2011, ESS gave out 19,158 scholarship awards to students from poor rural families in China. These were targeted toward students in primary, junior, and senior secondary vocational schools and colleges.

In 1998, the Organization of Chinese American Women embarked on a regular program of partnering with ESS. Since then, close to eight hundred scholarship awards were given to needy rural girl students in fifteen provinces: Xinjiang, Qinghai, Gansu, Ningxia, Heilongjiang, Inner Mongolia, Guizhou, Sichuan, Tibet, Yunnan, Hunan, Chongqing, Guangxi, Liaoning, and Henan. (Table 1 shows how the FARS was distributed among students through ESS in the fifteen provinces). The parents of these girls are mostly semiliterate and cannot afford to send their daughters to school.

Initial donations from OCAW and multiyear funds have been generously donated by OCAW chapters and individual members, families, and organizations.

Over the past fifteen years, each of the OCAW–related donors has received a feedback package, including receipts, school transcripts, and a thank-you letter from their respective aided students.

What the ESS/FARS has given to those children is not only financial support but also care and concern from the community at large. It serves as a catalyst that helps to sustain the dreams of these children, their families, and their home villages. Seeing their dreams fulfilled is the greatest reward for our ESS sponsors and volunteers.

## OCAW's Twenty-Second Anniversary Award Gala

OCAW's Twenty-Second Anniversary Award Gala and Mother's Day Salute Banquet was held on April 30, 1999, at the Fairview Park Marriott Hotel, Virginia. It honored Kultida Woods as OCAW's Mother of the Year and International Mother of the Year; Dinah Eng, columnist of *Bridges*, Gannett News Services, received OCAW's Leadership Award; and Grace Lee, designer and fashion show producer, received OCAW's Community Service Award.

Mrs. Woods was joined by her husband, Earl Woods, the best-selling author of *Training a Tiger,* and their son, Tiger Woods, the 1997 Master's golf champion.

The mistresses of ceremonies were Maureen Bunyan, ABC, WJLA, anchor; Shari Chen Macias, NBC, WRC, reporter/anchor; and Karen Palting, WNVC, producer. Live entertainment for the evening was presented by the Madison Chinese Dance Academy and the Tai Cultural Group. A surprise donation to OCAW's Scholarship for Middle School Girls in rural China was announced at the end of the event by the chairman of the Tiger Woods Foundation, Earl Woods.

## OCAW's 1999 National Conference: Sybil Kyi

From September 11 to 13, 1999 OCAW celebrated its biennial National Conference jointly with OCAW's Hawai'i Chapter's Tenth Anniversary at the Royal Hawaiian Hotel in Honolulu on the island of O'ahu. The theme

OCAW's Twenty-second Anniversary Awards Gala and Mother's Day Salute: Kultida Woods honored as OCAW 1999 Woman of the Year and International Mother of the Year; joined by her husband Earl Woods and their son Tiger Woods.

of the celebration was "Celebrating Our Legacy: A Kick-off to the New Millennium." We asked Sybil Kyi to write about that celebration. Like the other writers, she set about interviewing committee chairpersons and attendees of the conference who were available. Sybil's story follows.

> It all began when Anita Wong received a phone call in November 1988 from Julia Chang Bloch. Bloch was invited by then Hawai'i governor John Waihe'e to be a speaker at the Governor's Congress on Hawai'i's International Role held at the Hilton Hawaiian Village on December 6–7, 1988, and cosponsored by the University of Hawai'i and the East-West Center. Bloch asked if Anita could call together a group of Chinese women who may be interested in helping to start an OCAW chapter in Hawai'i for a meeting during her visit there. Anita, the incoming 1989 president of the Associated Chinese University Women (ACUW), a highly respected Chinese woman's organization in Hawai'i, arranged the meeting at the King Tsin Restaurant. Thirty-two ladies, most from the Executive Board of ACUW, attended that dinner meet-

ing, thanks to Blossom Y. Tyau's sense of history, for keeping that sign-in sheet all these years.

Also, in 1988, after Yeu-Tsu Margaret Lee, M.D., moved to Honolulu, Pauline W. Tsui asked her to consider establishing a Hawaii Chapter. Dr. Lee was a vibrant past president of OCAW's Los Angeles Chapter. She earned her M.D. degree cum laude in 1961 from Harvard Medical School, specializing in general and tumor surgery.

With the encouragement of Bloch and Tsui, six months later the Hawai'i Chapter was organized, and the OCAW National Board unanimously approved the new chapter in July 1989. Dr. Margaret Lee was nominated and elected as the first president of the Hawai'i Chapter of OCAW. The National Board asked the new Hawai'i Chapter to do two things: (1) double their number of members by having every member reach out for a new member and (2) send a delegation to the OCAW National Convention in Washington, D.C., to be held October 26–28, 1989, so they could interact with the national leadership and meet and learn how other chapters operate. The Hawai'i delegation also prepared to extend Hawai'i's aloha hospitality to the mainland women of OCAW. They took visitor and business conference information brochures, as well as exotic island snacks and flower leis. The Hawai'i delegation extended an invitation to hold a future biennial national meeting in Honolulu. The board was impressed by the Hawai'i presentation, and they voted unanimously to hold a future national biennial convention in Hawai'i. The 1989 Hawai'i delegation that went to Washington, D.C., included Christine Ling, Anita Wong, Lisa Lai, Janice Ching Yee, Rosie Chang, and Olivia Au. When they returned, they reported the warm reception and exciting events they experienced at the OCAW National Convention and the possibility of holding a national OCAW conference in Hawai'i.

Several years later, the Hawai'i Chapter succeeded in more than doubling its membership, and a trophy was sent from the national OCAW to reward its achievement.

In 1999 the opportunity arose to combine both the Biennial National OCAW Conference and the Hawaii OCAW Chapter's Tenth Anniversary celebration. The leaders of the joint conference were Vicky Cayetano (Hawai'i's First Lady, wife of Governor Benjamin Cayetano), who served as honorary chairperson; 1999 Hawai'i Chapter president Rose Y. Lee; and cochairpersons Blossom Young Tyau and Yun Soong Chock Jim. They were assisted by a committee of sixteen Hawai'i Chapter members: Therese Chun, Phyllis Shea, Queenie Mow Chee,

September 11–13, 1999, combined conference of OCAW Hawai'i Chapter Tenth Anniversary with OCAW National Biennial Celebration, Honolulu, Hawai'i. *L to R:* Rose Y. Lee, 1999 Hawai'i Chapter president, Blossom Y. Tyau and Yun Soong Jim, conference cochairpersons, and First Lady Vicky Cayetano, wife of then governor, Benjamin J. Cayetano. Photo courtesy of Blossom Y. Tyau.

Christine Ling, Betty Loui, Rosie Chang, Sandra Hagen, Gladys Lee, Juanita Takara-Hu, Patricia Lau, Patricia Chong, Juliette Ling, Beatrice Yuh, Shirley Chung, Rena Young Ochse, and Vivian Young.

The two cochairpersons exemplify the first generation of professional working women in Hawai'i. Yun Soong Chock Jim was the OCAW Hawai'i Chapter president for the two years (1997–1998) preceding the conference, and she had several occasions to meet and greet national OCAW leaders. In 1998, Ambassador Julia Chang Bloch stopped over in Honolulu after a visit to China. Yun Soong called the leaders of Honolulu's Chinese organizations to meet Ambassador Bloch at a luncheon at the Dynasty II Restaurant in Ward Warehouse. The ambassador shared her vision for expanding academic collaboration between Chinese and American universities. Yun Soong, the consummate educator, strongly supported this vision, especially in science education.

Yun Soong Chock Jim was born in Hilo, Hawai'i, the youngest

child and third daughter of ten children in a family that owned several business enterprises. Early in her life she developed an attitude of "can do" that became synonymous with her name. That spirit infused her life and her education career of thirty-five years as an award-winning science teacher in biology and chemistry. Her leadership in many community organizations ranged from president of the Lyon Arboretum Association to serving as a trustee for the United Chinese Society, which honored her in 1982 as its Model Chinese Mother. She was also honored as an outstanding biology teacher by the University of Hawai'i College of Education and McKinley High School; by the American Association of Retired Persons (AARP); and by the U.S.–China Peoples' Friendship Association, for which she served as a director.

Yun Soong was influenced by her six older brothers, all of whom pursued science fields. Two became medical doctors, two were dentists, and one each was in optometry and pharmacy. Yun Soong earned her bachelor's and master's degrees in biology from the University of Chicago. She met her husband, Dr. Vernon Jim, at the University of Chicago, where he was in medical school. After he graduated from medical school in 1944, they were married. The next day he enlisted in the U.S. Army, in which he served as a flight surgeon for three years. Yun Soong returned to Hilo, where their first two daughters were born. After Dr. Jim's military service ended, he and Yun Soong, now with four daughters, moved to Chicago for his further medical training at the University of Chicago and then to Minnesota in 1954 to enable Dr. Jim to study ophthalmology and plastic surgery at the Mayo Clinic; he later received board certification in both ophthalmology and reconstructive surgery. They returned to Hawai'i in 1956, where Yun Soong began her teaching career and Dr. Jim set up his practice. In their retirement years, they have experienced traveling adventures in places such as New Guinea and Antarctica. Most of all, they have continually and generously given their time and energies to local civic, social, and education causes. For their remarkably long history of service, the United Chinese Society honored both as Citizens of the Year.

Blossom Young Tyau was mistress of ceremonies for the conference program. Through her business network of friends, she arranged the most prestigious venue in Honolulu for the conference—the Royal Hawaiian Hotel—and secured dynamic local conference speakers. Blossom's career of over forty years as a travel and public relations manager prepared her well to become an outstanding community consultant for many social and philanthropic events.

Blossom was born and raised on Maui, the sixth of seven children. World War II and marriage interrupted her college years, and in 1949 she was offered a job with American President Lines (APL) that was to change her life. APL provided services to the University of Hawai'i and the East-West Center's foreign students, with Blossom as liaison and coordinator. She later joined the Friends of the East-West Center and served actively on its board. She also became a member of the East-West Center Foundation Board of Directors and served for eight years on the University of Hawai'i's Advisory Council for the College of Arts and Sciences.

Blossom's professional affiliations are numerous and varied and cover many decades and causes, including culture and the arts, commerce associations, and youth and eldercare programs. The Palolo Chinese Home bestowed on her the Distinguished Volunteer Service Award in a tribute dinner event called "Celebrating Community Volunteerism: A Lifetime of Service." The travel industry recognized Blossom's contributions in the Distinguished Woman of the Spirit Award, and the International Federation of Women's Travel Organizations gave her an honorary lifetime membership. The Travel Women of Hawai'i recognized Blossom as its first Most Outstanding Member. At its eightieth anniversary celebration, the Chinese Women's Club of Honolulu awarded her the club's Most Outstanding Member Award. She is regarded by many as a virtual ambassador plenipotentiary to a long list of Honolulu's civic and business organizations, and OCAW is privileged to have her as a member.

Blossom characterized the three days (September 11–13) of the 1999 national joint conference as a milestone for the Hawai'i Chapter. It signified the importance of Hawai'i as a place where women who excel in professional, business, and public service careers receive recognition for their accomplishments. On the second day, Blossom conducted the speakers' program, where the Governor's Proclamation for the Conference was presented by First Lady Vicky Cayetano. OCAW Distinguished Service Awards were bestowed on retired U.S. senator Hiram Leong Fong and his wife, Ellyn Lo Fong; on Sau Ung Loo Chan, Esq., the first Asian woman attorney to practice law in Hawai'i and who made a major contribution in working for the reentry of immigrant Chinese to the United States; and on Ah Quon McElrath, an eloquent spokeswoman, respected labor union activist, and social worker who was an iconic leader for social justice in Hawai'i, especially in advocating for the fair treatment of underprivileged people.

The distinguished panelists who spoke in the morning program on "Politics, Prose and Press" included moderator Jeanie F. Jew, 1999 National OCAW president; Ruby G. Moy, director of the U.S. Commission on Civil Rights; Sandra Oshiro, news media director for the *Honolulu Advertiser;* and Sondra Seba, who represented the White House Office for Women's Initiatives and Outreach. Blossom pointed out that First Lady Hillary Rodham Clinton sent a letter of congratulations to the OCAW Hawai'i Chapter that offered this insightful observation: "The fortunes of women are inextricably tied to the fortunes of our communities. If women flourish, then the entire community flourishes."

The third and last day of the 1999 biennial national conference began with a field trip to Senator Fong's Plantation and Gardens on the Windward or northeast side of O'ahu and ended with a reception and entertainment at Washington Place, the former home of the governor of Hawai'i and now a state museum and a site for state functions.

CHAPTER 4

# THE NEW MILLENNIUM
## 2000 THROUGH 2009

OCAW held its twenty-third Anniversary Award Dinner and Mother's Day Salute on May 13, 2000. It was cohosted by Ambassador Chan Heng Chee of Singapore at her Embassy in Washington, D.C.

The five 2000 Women of the Year honorees who received OCAW awards were as follows: Betty Tung, first lady of Hong Kong, received the 2000 International Woman of the Year Award; Nancy Chin-Lee, artist and president, Sino-American Lion Club, received the Mother of the Year Award; Faith Lee Breen, Ph.D., professor of management and deputy director of Gates Millennium Scholarship, received the Leadership Award; Elizabeth Fong, computer specialist and senior advocate, received the Community Service Award; and Pauline W. Tsui, cofounder of OCAW, received the Lifetime Achievement Award. Tsui's vision and tenacity have made OCAW the nation's largest Asian Pacific American women's group in the United States.

The evening opened with a panel on "Politics, Press and People," with speakers Ellen Yan, Laura Efurd, deputy assistant to the president and deputy director of the White House Office of Public Liaison, and Anna Chennault, chairperson, Council for International Cooperation.

Live entertainment was provided by Opera International on Broadway, with Bai Hai Bo and Muriel Hom, and the lion dance was performed by members of the Tai Yim Kung-Fu School.

On May 18, 2001, OCAW held its twenty-fourth Anniversary Award Dinner and Mother's Day Salute at the National Archives and Record Administration, honoring Dr. Franklin Odo, Smithsonian Institution; Suzanne Haddad, the Autry Museum of Western Heritage; Raymond A. Moxley, the National Archives and Records Administration; Beulah Quo, actress and community activist; and Lisa See, author, *On Gold Mountain.*

The day started with a tour of the Smithsonian Institution's "On Gold Mountain: A Chinese American Experience" exhibit, led by author Lisa See, followed by a dinner and ending with an exclusive night viewing of the Three Charters of Freedom in the Rotunda of the National Archives. The Three Charters of Freedom are the Declaration of Independence, the Constitution of the United States, and the Bill of Rights.

The event's general chairpersons were Jeanie F. Jew and Pauline W. Tsui. Cochair was Henriette Levy; dinner chair was Joanne Wang; and master of ceremonies at the reception was Mil Arcega, anchor and news reporter, NBC4-TV.

OCAW's Mother's Day event on May 4, 2002, entitled "Motherhood without Boundaries," was partnered with the Families with Children from China (FCC), Capital Area, and the Chinese Community Church, Washington, D.C., at the National Zoo. The program began with a tour of the zoo from the Panda House Terrace and ended with a lunch, where a Special Recognition Award was presented to FCC president Carol Colbeth. The chair of this event was Ruby G. Moy.

OCAW's twenty-fifth Anniversary National Conference and Silver Jubilee, "Smart Women: Path to Success," was held at the Reid Foundation Manor, Washington, D.C. This was followed by a Silver Jubilee Banquet at the beautiful Twin Oaks Estate on October 19, 2002.

Keynote speaker for the conference was the Honorable Chiling Tong, deputy assistant secretary for Asia and the Pacific, U.S. Department of Commerce. The workshop titles were as follows:

- Path to Success
- Path to Power: Inside the Government
- Path to Health: Achieving Physical and Financial Health
- Path to Arts and Literature: Face to Face with Artists and Author

The luncheon speaker was Faith Lee Breen, Ph.D., a management consultant who spoke on "Emotional Intelligence."

Sarah Lee, correspondent for NBC News and MSNBC, served as mistress of ceremonies. Presentation of the 2002 OCAW Mother of the Year Award went to Cora Mok. As for the Appreciation Awards, Teresa Ma accepted for the Herman Lissner Foundation; Dr. Eddie Wei accepted for the Li Foundation; and Pauline W. Tsui accepted the Twenty-Five Years of Exceptional Service Award.

Entertainment was provided by Yi-cheng Lin, baritone, and Linda Devine and Pin-Huey Wang, pianists. Chair of the banquet was Faith Lee

Breen, Ph.D., and the committee members were Sandy Taylor and Corinna Shen.

## OCAW's Accounting System by Margaret Wu

In 2002, OCAW's accounting system was professionally established by Margaret Wu, a financial director and an accountant (retired). She trained every staff member in using the system and checked and corrected every financial report and preparation of tax returns to ensure OCAW's no error products. OCAW deeply appreciates her years of voluntary assistance. Here is Margaret's story.

> When Pauline (founding president of OCAW) mentioned that OCAW needed volunteer help in 1999 concerning the office accounting system, personal computers had already become ubiquitous. Consequently, numerous accounting software programs for individuals and organizations of all sizes had become available at reasonable prices.
>
> After visits and meetings at the office, Pauline and the office manager explained the requirements and needs of the organization. So, I recommended the use of QuickBooks for OCAW. That accounting software was easy to learn and flexible for the various types of reporting they did, and in addition it was not too complicated to install or to maintain.
>
> The plan was that I would set the system up for them to keep records routinely and be available to answer questions and go to the office periodically to oversee payroll tax reporting and the preparation of the year-end accounting package for the accountants to complete the federal and state tax returns. For over a decade, this was exactly what transpired.
>
> Besides the routine of their accounting practices, there are some highlights and facts about OCAW's funding and accounting system that are worth mentioning briefly here.
>
> One highlight is that the national office of OCAW was managing many important programs of different kinds and purposes and that it was a 501 (C) (3) not-for-profit organization. As such, OCAW was under strict government requirements to disclose all the financial transactions involved in the programs and functions of the organization. Noncompliance could result in the loss of the tax-exempt status. The Opera International Program, under the capable and untiring leadership of Mimi Hom, was one of the largest, most successful, and highest

budgeted of all OCAW programs. The accounting for this very complicated undertaking had to conform to the additional requirements of government and tax reporting. Therefore, the Opera International funds have been kept in separate bank accounts and not comingled with OCAW's general operating bank account.

Another general highlight is that OCAW has enjoyed the financial support of many over the years. But the largest donation was from the trust created by Mrs. Ruth Kuo's estate. Her legacy was a generous endowment for educational grants and scholarships. When OCAW received the sizable funding from the trust in 2006, audited financial statements were required for reporting to the Maryland secretary of state on the *Maryland State Annual Report.* So a separate accounting firm of CPAs was retained to conduct the audit. The accounting system and, more importantly, the well-organized and immaculate records kept by Pauline and the office manager, facilitated the accountants' tasks to proceed quickly and successfully. In 2007, OCAW received additional sizable donations from the trust and from a beneficiary of this trust. These donations comprised virtually all the assets of OCAW.

On the human resources side, I have worked with many wonderfully efficient staff members at OCAW. The first one did not have any former accounting training but quickly learned to use QuickBooks. The last person I worked the longest with was really conscientious and eager to learn accounting and the applications of accounting computer software. We worked hard and well together and became good friends.

In conclusion, during the first decade of this, the twenty-first century, I had the opportunity to observe firsthand the hard work and monetary donations Pauline and all other volunteers contributed to the organization. They are inspirational and great role models for us who had the privilege to work with them.

## OCAW's Twenty-Seventh Anniversary National Conference by Cynthia Chang, Jean Chen, Anne Hu, Dorothy Lee and Ai-Chu Wang

OCAW's twenty-seventh Anniversary National Conference was held August 7–8, 2004, at the Crowne Plaza, San Jose, California. Its theme was "Empowering Women for the 21st Century." The mayor of Saratoga, California, the Honorable Ann Waltonsmith, proclaimed August 7, 2004, as the city's support of OCAW Day.

OCAW's Silicon Valley Chapter (SVC) hosted the conference, and they did an outstanding job. We contacted Alice Chiou, 2012 OCAW–SVC president, and asked if the chapter would like to write about the 2004 conference.

> OCAW's twenty-seventh Anniversary National Conference, August 7–8, 2004, which we, the OCAW–Silicon Valley Chapter hosted, was a lot of work for all, but we felt it was very worthwhile not only for us who labored to plan and execute the plan but for the attendees as well. We thought the theme for the conference, "Empowering Women for the 21st Century," was very appropriate. Many out-of-town members flew in the night before and joined local members for a welcome dinner. On August 7, the day began with breakfast at the Crowne Plaza for a general membership meeting so all members could get acquainted with each other. We discovered each chapter had different emphases in serving Chinese American women. Members mingled and networked among chapters during lunch.
>
> Conference workshops and their leaders for the first day's program (August 7) after lunch were as follows:
>
> 1. Empowering Women By Exploring Leadership Characteristics: led by OCAW national president Rosetta Lai
> 2. Spinal Health And You: led by Wendy Chuang, D.C.
> 3. Empowering Women for the 21st Century: a panel discussion moderated by Anne Hu; the panelists were as follows:
>
>    Cynthia Chang, trustee, Los Gatos-Saratoga High School District; Cecilia Lee Chang, president, Justice for New Americans; Dr. Josephine Ong-Hawkins, president, Asian Americans for Community Involvement; and Lie-Szu Juang, director, Taiwan Semiconductor Manufacturing Company North America
>
> "An Evening of Celebration" was the theme for evening program. Awards were presented to the following:
>
> 1. Jeanie and Robert Jew, OCAW Pillar Awards
> 2. Cynthia Chang, OCAW Community Service Award
> 3. Cecilia Lee Chang, OCAW Leadership Award
>
> The OCAW–Silicon Valley Chapter held an installation of officers ceremony. Presentation of the OCAW Scholarship was awarded to Da-

vid Luoh for the Presidential Classroom Program. Youth Achievement Awards were given to Cynthia Chuang, Tiffany Jon, Jessica Li, David Luoh, Kate Wang, and Randy Yuan. The winners were all local high school junior and senior students.

Dinner entertainment of Broadway musical selections was provided by Hank Gioia and Grace Sams. After-dinner entertainment was provided by a children's fashion show, a teen's fashion show, an adult fashion show, Chinese folk dance, tap dance, jazz dance, hip hop, Chinese popular song, and a cappella singing. The evening program was successfully concluded with karaoke and social dance.

The OCAW–Silicon Valley Chapter offers unique fashion shows for OCAW members and their teenage children as an annual event. Thus the show was integrated into the national conference as the finale. Models go through choreographed routines showing casual wear/school wear, career wardrobe, and formal wear segments. Thus they have an opportunity to build self-confidence and self-esteem. In addition, two high school students work as emcees for the fashion show so they can learn public speaking skills and speaking off the cuff when needed. The OCAW–Silicon Valley Chapter is fortunate to have local scholarship donors as well as the Presidential Classrooms Scholarships funded by national OCAW in Washington, D.C. each summer.

On August 8, there was a breakfast gathering at Crowne Plaza. It was almost like a farewell party. Two days were truly too short for getting together. After breakfast, some out-of-town members joined a bus tour to a scenic Monterey seventeen-mile drive tour before they flew home. About two hundred OCAW national and chapter members and their family attended this two-day event.

Tracy Lee was the 2004 OCAW–SVC Chapter president. Mistress of ceremonies was Pei-chun Liao, the Mandarin anchorwoman for KTSF. The conference chair was Ai-chu Wang, a past president of OCAW and committee members were Cynthia Chang, Chia-Huei Chen, Jean Chen, Samantha Cheng, Moli Fries, Monica Hsiao, Anne Hu, Aileen Kao, Katy Wang, and Tracy Lee. Organizing a national conference was not an easy task. We put it off for many years, however, we felt it was a history-making event for our Chapter, and the bonding of sisterhood in OCAW makes us all feel stronger and appreciative of who we are.

Cynthia Chang, OCAW–SVC past president, 1991–1993 and 2005–2007, has been an active member of the chapter since its founding in 1986. She is very proud of what the chapter has accomplished

OCAW Silicon Valley Chapter, founded in 1986, leaders/members, goal-focused, cohesive group; *back row, L to R:* Tracy Lee, Anne Hu, Cynthia Chang, Ai-chu Wang, Jean Chen, Tammy Wang, Sue Wu, Chin-The Cheng; *front row, L to R:* Kathy Wang, Samantha Cheng, Chia-Huei Chen, Esther Lee, Dorothy Lee, Sophia Yang, Monica Hsiao, Alice Chiou, Rose Cheng.

and remembered that OCAW–SVC's first fashion show was held on July 12, 1986 with Sussana Su as the director. Our main purpose was to bring awareness of women's image to the forefront with appropriate dressing and style. On June 27, 1987, OCAW–SVC presented its first youth scholarship and fashion show. Both have become a tradition of OCAW–SVC as an annual event and which also serve as an effective membership drawing tool.

Alice Chiou, Cynthia Chang, Dorothy Lee, Jean Chen, Ai-chu Wang, Anne Hu, and Tracy Lee, as well as all past OCAW–SVC presidents, believe that following goals, are not only for the membership of their chapter, but are also important for all women. Following, are our Chapter's basic goals:

1. Integrate Chinese American Women into the mainstream of American society.

2. Improve Chinese American image by increasing our self-respect, self-confidence, and self-esteem.
3. Exchange cultural background to eliminate racial and cultural misunderstanding.
4. Address a variety of issues and concerns facing Chinese American women today.
5. Help Asian immigrants to understand and adapt to the American society while keeping what's good in their traditional culture.
6. Work cooperatively with other organizations with similar goals.

## ASIAN AMERICAN WOMEN'S LEADERSHIP DEVELOPMENT PROGRAM: ROSETTA LAI

During May 9–13, 2005, OCAW teamed up with the Center for Creative Leadership (CCL) of Greensboro, North Carolina, in conducting the Asian American Women's Leadership Development Program. Rosetta Lai, developer, producer, and trainer and OCAW national president 2003–2008, discusses the content of this training program below.

OCAW appreciates the partnership with CCL, the number-one-ranked leadership institute in the United States, enabling OCAW's establishment of the first Asian American Women's Leadership Development Program.

OCAW was also delighted to discover great interest and endorsement from U.S. Fortune 500 companies as well as from government agencies and nonprofit organizations in developing Asian American Women's senior leadership. The entities that sent their attendees were the following:

1. Marriott Corporation
2. U.S. National Institutes of Health
3. U.S. Department of Veteran's Affairs
4. Two OCAW chapter presidents
5. State Farm Insurance
6. Motorola Inc.
7. American Legacy Foundation

An example of the effectiveness of this training program was seen by the result of one of the nineteen graduates' practice of learning to use a self-promotion strategy, saying she is responsible, reliable, and loyal to her company. Immediately upon her return to her work, she also discussed with her superior about her career future and received a promotion within a month. Many of the graduates requested forming an annual meeting to continue networking and support of each other.

Following is Ms. Lai's content brief of the Asian American Women's Leadership Development Program.

> *Introduction:* I conceived of the idea for this program when I became the national president of OCAW in 2003. I wanted to make a signature contribution to OCAW based on the corporate experiences I have had that would also meet the needs of the members of OCAW. U.S. corporations have recognized the importance of talent and leadership among their executive ranks and have invested in their grooming and development. Elaborate systems and processes are in place, and general managers are rewarded for their development of talent besides generating profits and successes for their business units. I have met amazing women at OCAW and am aware of the barriers that block a number of them from fulfilling their leadership potential. Some of these barriers can be overcome by leadership development programs. So I researched various programs in this area and settled on a partnership with the Center of Creative Leadership (CCL), headquartered in Greensboro, North Carolina, to develop an Asian American Women's Leadership Development Program.
>
> *Key Objective of the Program:* The key objective of the program is to empower Asian American women to direct their lives with intelligent choices and confidence to overcome barriers inherent in our identity of being American, Asian, and female.
>
> *Audience:* The audience is Asian American women in senior-level management positions.
>
> *Focus:* This program brings powerful personal assessment and feedback elements together with research-based content that delves into issues and perceptions surrounding Asian American women's work and leadership experiences. It is designed to provide opportunities for reflection and improvement of leadership capabilities. In addition, it offers a secure forum for Asian American women to clarify strengths and developmental issues and to work with models of power and influence to explore the choices and tradeoffs they face as Asian American women juggling personal and professional objectives. The program stimulates a process of growth that will allow each participant to take responsibility for her own leadership development and success.
>
> *Program Implementation:* Since this was the first external and in-

dependent leadership development program unaffiliated with any corporation or organization, it took one year to market it nationally among major U.S. corporations. It took another six months for me to work with CCL managers and facilitators to custom design the program based on the framework of executive development at CCL.

The program was attended by nineteen high- and mid-level executives with high potential talent from seven U.S. corporations and government agencies. They traveled to Greensboro, North Carolina, for this five-day program. The secluded and beautiful campus offered an ideal environment for reflection, networking, and learning. Following is a summary of comments by the participants describing what they have taken away from the program:

- Gained a full and honest picture of strengths and developmental needs with prioritization.
- Developed the skills of giving and receiving constructive feedback.
- Learned strategies for using power and influence more effectively.
- Learned how to overcome the biases and discomforts associated with exercising political know-how.
- Made new choices for investment of personal energy based on examination of tradeoffs and rewards.
- Learned how to lead with authenticity, clarifying personal values and their fit within the organizational culture.
- Set goals and developed strategies for improving leadership capabilities.

## OCAW's 2006 Bylaws Amendment

During 2005 and 2006, Virginia Cheung, Esq., the OCAW National Board's pro bono legal advisor, finalized OCAW's 2006 Bylaws Amendment with the assistance of Josephine Lo, Esq., and Suzy Hung, Esq. In addition to these three, the committee of five consisted of National President Rosetta Lai and Acting Executive Director Pauline W. Tsui. They toiled many, many hours to accomplish this difficult task.

The final draft was unanimously passed by the general membership. OCAW appreciates the countless hours of voluntary services provided by the three attorneys and the continuing legal counseling of Virginia Cheung since the earlier years of OCAW.

2005 Asian-American Women's Leadership Development Program, nineteen attendees, four instructors. *First row, L to R:* Diane Lam, Hong Quach, Phanny Schinner, Audrey Ogawa Johnson, Shari Lent, Rosetta Lai lead instructor; Sharon Ting, instructor; Judy Liu. *Second row, L to R:* Ancella Livers, instructor; Laura Hamasaka, Suzy Hung, Yvette Karaba, Brenda Sumberg, instructor; Pavarthy Bhaskaran, Christina Chan. *Back row, L to R:* Mandy Kam, Carolyn Wong, Linda Weidman, Maria Uy, Cynthia Chang, Judy Chen, Deepti Arora, Yuan Liu.

## OCAW's Thirtieth Anniversary

OCAW celebrated its Thirtieth Anniversary on August 4–5, 2007, at the Marriott Residence Inn. Its theme was "Strategic Planning for OCAW as a National Asian American Women's Organization." A dinner at the Penang Malaysian Restaurant and an operatic concert at the Music Center at Strathmore in Bethesda, Maryland, were enjoyed by all.

The objectives for the Strategic Planning were as follows:

1. Review of the mission of OCAW against the changing needs of Asian American women in the last thirty years
2. Awareness of the segmentation of Asian American women by ethnicity, education, socioeconomic background, and time/generation in the United States
3. Review of the current structure of OCAW as a federation of local chapters with a national office based in Bethesda, Maryland
4. Review of various options for the structure of OCAW, considering Pauline W. Tsui's retirement from the board and as acting director
5. Recommendations for a desired organizational structure, recognizing the current structure of a national office and outlying chapters, yet not relying on that same structure

Conference chair was Rosetta Lai. Conference committee members were Pauline W. Tsui and Virginia Woo. The Operatic Concert was produced by Muriel Hom.

In September 2007, Faith Lee Breen, Ph.D., was elected national president and Janet Biermann was appointed national executive director. Linda Devine was appointed editor and producer of OCAW's e-newsletter.

## PRESIDENTIAL CLASSROOM SCHOLARSHIP PROGRAM: CHELSEA LO

Chelsea Lo, OCAW 2008 Presidential Classroom Scholarship recipient. Photo courtesy of Josephine Lo, Esq.

In August 2008, Miss Chelsea Lo, from Maryland, was awarded a full OCAW Presidential Classroom scholarship to attend a one-week-long program in Washington, D.C. This is a long-standing OCAW scholarship program for Chinese American senior high school students. Students are selected from a rigorous set of criteria so they can receive full benefit from what was described as an "extraordinary academic and leadership development experience." With Chelsea's permission, it is our pleasure to present her Presidential Classroom Critique Essay.

Thank you very much, OCAW, for supporting me and giving me a wonderful opportunity to learn more about my country. I attended the special July 4 Presidential Scholars program, hosted by Presidential Classroom, with the financial assistance (full scholarship) of OCAW. I took a lot away from the program and I feel that I am now a more cultured student and a better-informed citizen. Presidential Classroom arranged a variety of invigorating activities, including crossfire sessions, seminars with important speakers, a mock Congress, and field trips to Washington, D.C., and Philadelphia.

Each day was long, starting as early as 5 a.m. and running as late as 11 p.m. While it was grueling at times, I think that Presidential Classroom tried its best to squeeze in as many enriching experiences as possible so that students got their money's worth.

The site director said that our program was one of the smallest groups with only sixty students, which I found unsettling at first because I had just attended a ten-day conference in New York with more than double that number. I soon bonded, however, with my caucus (we were split into two caucuses of thirty students each), with which I traveled and prepared for the mock Congress. I loved the two-caucus setup because I was able to bond with and get to know members of my own caucus, while still having plenty of chances to mingle with students from the other caucus.

Every time we went on site visits (such as the National Air and Space Museum, monuments at the Mall, Pentagon City Mall, Liberty Bell, Philadelphia Constitution Center, and Baltimore Harbor), there was ample social time, which created a healthy balance between fun and work, the latter being the bulk of our daily schedules. I loved that Presidential Classroom trusted us to be individual (I was pleasantly surprised to find that I, at age sixteen, was one of the younger participants; a number of students were graduated high school seniors) and responsible, giving us strict report times and boundaries, which were nevertheless loose enough that we did not feel constrained.

During the course of the week, we had two crossfire sessions in which we discussed and debated ethical and political questions of the day. In my first crossfire, the group got into a rather tense debate over the role of religion in public places. I did not really enjoy that crossfire very much because one of the girls in the group was not open-minded, which I think is crucial to a healthy debate. Being open-minded does not mean one is overly willing to change one's beliefs or easily swayed, it merely means that one can accept that others disagree and that one will not get worked up over it. The girl, however, did not really want to hear what others had to say, and even when agreeing with someone her tongue was sharp. That, of course, was not Presidential Classroom's fault.

My second crossfire, however, left me enthralled. The staff moderator, a member of the armed forces, strayed from the list of questions he was given. He moved the discussion along the tangents that it was veering off into rather than pulling us back to the list; it was the best decision he could have made. Every person in that room had a strong opinion and was willing to listen to his/her peers. We discussed the Supreme Court's recent habeas corpus decision, the direction of education in the modern world (one girl came from South Korea and she shared interesting observations), standardized testing, women in the military, and abortion. I am sure that we went into several other mini-topics, each with its own fascinating insights, but I cannot remember them now. Each crossfire session had about fifteen students, a group that was small enough to be intimate and to allow everyone a chance to speak, yet large enough to be diverse.

We also had several keynote speakers with whom we were given question/answer sessions. Speakers included a professor from American University, a U.S. Marine Corps general, a member of FECA (Federal Election Campaign Act), and our very own counselors (a boy/girl pair of counselors per caucus; the two ladies were teachers, and the two men were both members of the U.S. armed forces). My favorite was the professor from American University, Ed Smith. He was amazing. With a visage resembling both Einstein and Frederick Douglass, he expounded upon the power of language and the role of color in society. He was the most down-to-earth professor I have ever heard, with a sense of humor that tickled the stomachs of every generation in that room. I do not think there was a single mouth that did not involuntarily twitch with laughter that night. At one point, he was rattling on in an endearing way about the power of words and decided to illustrate with a famous story from the Bible, where Jesus saved Mary from villagers who were stoning her. With each reflective pause between Professor Smith's words, I grew increasingly uncomfortable, not because I am not a Christian but because I was afraid that the professor's charm was wearing off with the young, defiant minds sitting around me who might not be Christians. I wanted so badly for everybody in that room to like him because I liked him so much! Professor Smith was describing how Mary was running from her pursuers and crying for help from Jesus, and I thought that he had gone too far. But then he said something unexpected: "Mary cried for help from Jesus, and he came! She wanted help, and Jesus just happened to be there for her! I don't know what the heck he was doing—Jesus was at a 7-11 or something, I don't know—but he was there!" Immediately, the tense silence and restless fidgeting in the room exploded into raucous laughter. Everyone was turning to each other with their eyes crinkling in laughter. "Did you hear him? Ha ha, Jesus at a 7-11!" It was brilliance. We students were supposed to maintain our professionalism, sitting tall and rapt with attention. (Presidential Classroom was by far the most professional camp I have ever attended. The students were so responsible; I was really impressed and appreciative.) But I couldn't help pulling paper out of my notebook to scrawl down little insights that Prof. Smith had given me.

After the speech, one of our counselors asked us to rate Professor Smith on a scale of one to five (five being the best), and every student gave him either a four or a five. Our counselors had never asked us to rate speakers before, and therefore I believe they thought Professor Smith was special, too. Also, I believe that the students at Presidential Scholars did not just give fours or fives because of peer pressure; every student there was informed and had an opinion. Therefore, I do not think any student would have given Professor Smith a four if they really thought he had deserved a three.

Finally, the field trips were amazing. At the Constitution Center in Philadelphia, we got to see life-size statues of our founding fathers, a multimedia show on this country's roots called "Freedom Rising," really interesting information on American presidents, and voting. A few students were tearing up after the "Freedom Rising" show because they were so proud of the United States; I felt bad that I wasn't as deeply affected.

Later, however, I was wandering through the exhibit hall and came upon a large screen showing a short video of people taking the oath for American citizenship. I watched it three times; I loved seeing the African man kissing his American flag tie, the Chinese woman grinning infectiously, the Indian woman shaking her certificate with glee, the Caucasian man high-fiving his wife. I loved seeing people's faces; they are so telling.

For that same reason, I loved all of our field trips to the memorials (we saw many of the ones on the Mall as well as others scattered around D.C., such as the U.S. Air Force and U.S. Navy memorials). I live ten minutes away from D.C., but I rarely see these memorials, and I bet that I am among a great number of Washingtonians who take these memorials for granted. The last time I saw them was on a field trip in the sixth grade and maybe the eighth grade too. With Presidential Scholars, I was able to see the Korean War, Lincoln, World War II, Franklin Delano Roosevelt, and Jefferson memorials. I think the World War II Memorial was the most beautiful, but the Korean War Memorial was my favorite because of the evocative quality of the statues and the evident time and care that went into the etching of the faces that line the black granite wall of the memorial.

One of my counselors was a retired U.S. Marine Corps general, Dan—a really patriotic old guy. In his goodbye speech to us, he was telling us about how our peers (our age!) are going overseas to serve our duty as citizens for us. That made us all pretty stone faced. But then he pointed at the other male counselor, who was in his early twenties at most. And he said, "He's in the reserves on active duty. Do you know what that means? That means that any day, maybe even tomorrow, the army can call him up and say, 'Hey, man, we need you to serve,' and the next day, he'll be in Afghanistan on the front lines so you all can go to sleep in a safe bed. It's men like him that are fighting so that you can live in a democracy!" And then I cried. I didn't make any sound, but tears were running down my cheeks. Because you cannot just look at the counselor Dan was talking about—really think about how such a nice guy could be shipped overseas any day, how he's willing to be shipped overseas any day, how he could be killed while he is over there, how he will not come back—and not cry. It is just so brave. I will never have that kind of bravery, and I envy people who do have it. I give Presidential Classroom full credit for giving me all that emotion, because it introduced me to Dan (he has contacts, so I can send packages overseas to our soldiers!) and the other counselors; this program gave me the opportunity to appreciate our armed forces and encouraged me to be an American citizen.

At the end of the week, Presidential Classroom asked every student to develop a civic action plan for their community, and if we get it working we can write back to Presidential Classroom and get ourselves published. Presidential Classroom can help with supplies and contacts if we need them. But most importantly, we'll be making a difference. And we're not even twenty yet!

Since this is a critique essay, I guess I should add some critiques! I really don't have that many. The housing arrangements were a bit cramped, but they were comfortable, so I'm not going to complain. We had to pay for our own lunches each day, but the staff always provided us with free snacks at night in case we were hungry. The early wake-up times were necessary, so no complaint there. Throughout the preparation for our mock Congress, our group felt like there was not enough time and resources to do necessary research, but the actual mock Congress was phenomenal, even without the benefits of further research. Therefore, in retrospect, my sole complaint is no longer relevant. Every staff member was fun and enthusiastic, and scheduling ran like a well-oiled machine. Great job, Presidential Classroom!

## New Orleans Meetings: Betty Butz

OCAW's New Orleans Chapter has been hit hard by the recent hurricanes. Dr. Faith Lee Breen, OCAW National President took time from her busy calendar to visit the New Orleans Chapter on the last weekend of October 2009. On the evening of October 23, President Betty Butz, past president Lucy Chun, Ruby Verhoeven, and Faith had a wonderful meeting together. These women are very accomplished. For example, Betty Butz is a past president of the Ikebana International New Orleans Chapter; Lucy Chun is a very successful multimillion-dollar real estate broker; and Ruby Verhoeven is the owner of the Rose Manor Inn Bed & Breakfast. Discussion focused on the following issues:

1. Aging parents who need financial, emotional, and physical assistance
2. Married daughters who are trying to maintain a healthy marriage, family life, and career
3. Unmarried sons and daughters who are finding it difficult to become financially established and find a life partner who will commit to marriage
4. Obtaining reliable domestic help who will not "steal your husband"
5. Finding time to participate in nurturing activities suggested by OCAW National

The next day, Saturday, October 24, Dr. Breen met with OCAW's New Orleans Chapter at a general meeting in Kenner. The chapter shared with Dr. Breen several of the programs that it is supporting. For example, they are very involved with the local Chinese language school program and have branched out into martial arts. Dr. Breen suggested that they may also want to start sponsoring Tai Chi classes, because this is an intergenerational activity that has a lot of benefits, including stress management and enhanced concentration for learning. As part of their meeting, Dr. Breen talked about retirement planning:

- What does retirement mean to you and do you really want to retire?
- When should you retire?
- Where do you want to live and is this realistic?
- How much money will you need?

Dr. Breen also talked about OCAW's "Cycles of Life" project, honing in on its applicability to Chinese American women. Incidentally, Dr. Breen had talked about this project with the Maryland Chapter members on March 29, 2009, whose president was Christina Wong Poy.

New Orleans Chapter members were eager to learn more about the organization at the national level, such as the work of Opera International, the Presidential Classroom Scholarships Program, and the scholarship awards to girls in rural China. Dr. Breen inspired the group to support each other's aspirations and endeavors. Her caring words and gentle demeanor were a breath of fresh air after the recent devastating Hurricane Katrina. OCAW made a very generous donation to the chapter. Dr. Breen's visit invigorated members with new ideas.

To address the needs of the group, Betty Butz, chapter president 2008–2012, proposed a four-part program under the theme of "Personal Health Devotion." The four parts were organized under the topics of healthy foods, massage therapy, healing herbs, and healing words. Workshops were held on each topic. She recruited Guiqin Xiong and Yizhi Zhang, who were visiting from China, to serve as honorary health advisors. They were both trained in Chinese medicine in China.

The New Orleans Chapter continues to meet to address matters central to our mission of education and service. Some of the members are leaders in the Asian Pacific American Society, the Academy of Chinese Studies, the New Orleans Chinese Association, and the Asian Chamber of Commerce of Louisiana. Members support each other by sharing personal stories that are healing to the spirit and appealing to the mind.

We asked Betty to write a bit of the history of the Chinese in New Orleans, which includes how OCAW's New Orlean's Chapter got started. Her story follows.

> The earliest Chinese in the New Orleans area had mostly emigrated from coastal towns in China, and they spoke Cantonese. They operated small businesses, primarily in laundry service, restaurants, and shrimp processing. Today, New Orleans dried shrimp is sold in local Asian supermarkets, and wholesale frozen shrimp is available from Chinese American–owned processing facilities located in Lafitte,

Louisiana. Many of the descendants of this community and subsequent groups of immigrants have pursued academic and professional careers.

A Chinese Presbyterian Church was formed in 1882 in the Mid-City neighborhood of New Orleans to help immigrants learn English and acclimate to life in America. Services were conducted in Cantonese and in English. As the congregation grew, the church was relocated to Kenner in Jefferson Parish. Services were held in English, with simultaneous translations into Cantonese, Mandarin, and Taiwanese. It still serves as a welcoming portal for newcomers who wish to become connected in a new place. Sheriff Harry Lee (1932–2007) was a member. His daughter Cynthia Lee-Sheng was elected councilwoman of District 5 in Jefferson Parish in 2009.

Patricia Hew, ordained ruling elder and deacon of the Chinese Presbyterian Church in the 1980s, was a fourth-generation Chinese American and New Orleans native. Her great-grandfather, Chin Lin Sou (1836–1894), from Dongguan, Guangzhou, worked as a foreman in building the first transcontinental railroad from California to Colorado, eventually settling in the Denver area. Her grandmother Rose came to New Orleans with her husband in the late 1800s and raised a large family.

Pat Hew learned about the Organization of Chinese American Women while she attended an Asian American Education Association meeting in Washington, D.C. In 1989 she helped to form the New Orleans Chapter. The first president of the New Orleans Chapter was Shaie Mei Temple. She came to the United States as a student, became a nuclear engineer, and then worked in southern Louisiana. She started the New Orleans Chapter in December 1989 after meeting and discussing with Pauline W. Tsui at a White House meeting in Washington, D.C. Ms. Hew served as chapter president in the late 1990s. Two of the founding members, Tina Soong and Tai Chen Ho, remain active.

With the sponsorship of Deacon Hew, the New Orleans Chapter met frequently at the Chinese Presbyterian Church in Kenner. In 2003, there were thirty-seven members, most of whom were immigrants from Hong Kong, Taiwan, and mainland China. A few were locally born Chinese Americans, with one Vietnamese American member. Today the chapter has seventeen members of similar ethnic composition. Among them are active and retired small business owners and professionals, two hotel operators, a commercial real estate agent, a journalist, attorneys, and scientists.

The New Orleans story completes our presentation. We hope readers enjoyed this brief history of OCAW and the stories of the guest writers and will recommend this book to others who would like to know more about Chinese American women. Our book on the history of OCAW from 1977 through 2009 was written with the following three purposes in mind:

1. To professionally record OCAW's sustained, well-planned educational and social outreach programs to integrate Chinese American women into the mainstream of America's activities and programs during the last quarter of the twentieth century and first decade of the twenty-first century.
2. To give recognition to those who contributed to the accomplishments of OCAW.
3. To have this history available as study material in women's studies and ethnic-Asian studies programs throughout the United States of America, at least, and in selected parts of Asia.

# Appendix 1

## "Chinese American Women: A Brief History and Bibliography"

*Editor's note:* This report was funded by the Women's Education Equity Act Program, U.S. Department of Education, 1983. Project director was Pauline W. Tsui.

### Program Staff and Consultants

| | |
|---|---|
| Project Director | Pauline W. Tsui |
| Principal Program Consultant | Esther Chow, Ph.D. |
| Organization of Chinese American Women National Education Advisory Committee | Julia Chang Bloch<br>Lily Lee Chen<br>Freda Cheung, Ph.D.<br>Esther Chow, Ph.D.<br>Gladys Chang Hardy<br>Beverley Jung<br>Canta Pian<br>Betty Lee Sung, Ph.D.<br>Tina Sung<br>Margot Wei<br>Gwendolyn Wong<br>Esther Lee Yao, Ph.D. |
| Program Staff | Kwan Ming Koehler<br>Josephine Lo |
| Program Support Staff | Cindy Yee |

## PREFACE

The Organization of Chinese American Women (OCAW) was awarded a three-year grant by the Women's Educational Equity Act Program (WEEAP), U.S. Department of Education, in October 1980 to carry out its project. We began the project, entitled the Chinese American Women Educational Equity Program, by conducting a literature review on Chinese American women, particularly in education and employment. The purpose of the literature review was to replace ignorance, misinformation, and stereotypes about Chinese American women with an objective and accurate description of our past and present, including our origins, history, achievements, problems, and concerns.

OCAW first identified experts in the field and convened a National Education Advisory Committee. Under the guidance of the committee, and using the information it supplied, our project staff was able to lay the groundwork for the review. The input OCAW received from Dr. Esther Chow, a member of the advisory committee and the principal project consultant, was especially helpful in the development of a comprehensive listing of resource materials.

Initially, we planned to complete the material research within three months. However, the scarcity of published materials on the subject and the anticipation of up-to-date information soon to be supplied by the 1980 census persuaded us to extend our search to the full duration of the project. As we proceeded to compile and record materials, a formidable file gradually took shape. It was then that we decided to compose a select bibliography on Chinese American women in education and employment. Although the development of this bibliography was not part of our original proposal to WEEAP, and therefore not appropriated for in the budget, we managed to complete this extra task without any cost overruns. This was accomplished primarily with the aid of several computer searches. Databases we found to be particularly useful were the Educational Resources Information Center (ERIC), the National Clearinghouse on Mental Health, the Smithsonian Science Information Exchange, and the Library of Congress, as well as a variety of abstracts. Our biggest disappointment is still the lack of current relevant data. The 1980 census, a gold mine of information in many other ways, fails to tell us much about Chinese Americans as a group, let alone Chinese American women.

This work, entitled *Chinese American Women: A Brief History and Bibliography*, has been critiqued and evaluated by OCAW's Education Advisory Committee, the editorial staff of the WEEA Publishing Center, and a national review panel assembled by the Wellesley College Center for Research on Women. This book has been recommended for use by both Chinese and non-Chinese Americans who wish to understand Chinese American women better. It can serve as a reference source for teachers and school administrators in curriculum planning. Government personnel; Equal Employment Opportunity (EEO) offices at the local, state, and federal levels; counselors; and social workers will also find it to be useful. In short, *Chinese American Women: A Brief History and Bibliography* will be a valuable and unique addition to the collection of any library.

As project director of the Chinese American Women Educational Equity Program, I wish to thank everyone who has contributed to this work. My appreciation goes to members of OCAW's project staff, particularly, Ms. Kwan Ming Koehler, our project consultant; Dr. Esther Chow; members of the Education Advisory Committee; the editorial staff of the WEEA Publishing Center; and the Wellesley College Center's review panel. Our gratitude is due to the Women's Educational Equity Act Program, U.S. Department of Education, which funded OCAW's project and made this publication possible.

Pauline W. Tsui

## CHINESE AMERICAN WOMEN: A BRIEF HISTORY

Until very recently, little research has been conducted relating specifically to Chinese American women. As a consequence, the literature concerning this segment of the population is extremely limited.

Somewhat more has been written about the Chinese American in general, and still more about the "Asian American", a phrase conceived and used with increasing frequency since the Asian American movement took form in the late 1960s and spread to college campuses across the nation. Asian American is now generally understood to include Americans of Chinese, Japanese, Korean, Filipino, and Vietnamese descent, as well as Pacific Islanders.

The most telling points that emerge from a review of the available literature are: that there has been a dramatic increase in the number of Chinese females in the United States; (b) that Chinese American women have serious problems of underemployment and occupational segregation; and (c) that these problems result, in part, from institutional discrimination and the failure of the educational system to prepare Chinese American women to compete successfully in the job market.

There is general agreement by all sources about these inequities and about some recommendations to address the problems created by them.

Following are the salient details of the Chinese American woman's history of immigration and her current social and economic situation.

### *Cultural Background*

In order to arrive at any kind of clear understanding of the problems facing Chinese American women as they struggle to achieve educational and occupational parity in contemporary American society, it is first necessary to examine several subjects. They include the culture of the Chinese homeland, the pattern of immigration to the United States, the attitudes of the dominant population, and the current occupational and educational status of Chinese American women.

In the Confucian society of nineteenth century China, women were accorded distinctly inferior status, and had virtually no control over their own destinies. An infant girl was looked upon as another mouth to feed until such time as she could be married off. The birth of a boy was cause for celebration. During times of famine or extreme economic distress, infanticide of female offspring was common, and so was the selling of female children into household slavery, or worse, prostitution.

More affluent families might have cherished and pampered their daughters, but seldom did they give them any significant education; that was reserved for the sons. Instead, a girl was expected to perform domestic chores and to help care for younger siblings. Indeed, she was actively discouraged from developing talents or abilities that might prepare her for a career outside the home. Generally confined to home and hearth, a Chinese female was dependent on and subordinate to the males of the family: in childhood to her father and brothers; as a young woman, to her husband; and in old age, to her sons. Her marriage was arranged, often without regard to her wishes. She suffered abrupt separation from her own family thereafter, and enjoyed no property rights. Garrulousness and the failure to bear male children were grounds for divorce.

In short, throughout her life the Chinese woman was taught and expected to be passive, submissive to men, industrious, preferably not too intelligent, and most certainly not assertive. These attitudes, so deeply ingrained, were carried over to the new country and still persist, in varying degrees.

***Immigration and Settlement***

The pattern of early immigration and settlement has had far-reaching effects on the Chinese American communities of today. A great wave of emigration, most of it from the southeastern coastal provinces of China, took place in the second half of the nineteenth century. The historical coincidence of floods, famine, and revolution and the discovery of gold in California attracted thousands of Chinese, almost exclusively male, to America. The majority of these men left their wives and children behind, and often were separated from them for decades.

Chinese men came to work the mines, to build railroads, to toil in factories and fields, and to settle. But even before they arrived, they were preceded by negative, stereotyped images spread by British and American diplomats, and by merchants who were then plundering the tottering Manchu Empire. The United States was beginning to emerge as a world power and a mighty industrial nation, and the robber barons were eager to exploit this supply of cheap labor.

The general populace greeted the Chinese with suspicion and scorn. The economic depression of the 1870s created social unrest, and the new immigrants became everyone's scapegoats. Hostility exploded into mob violence that began in the mines of California and spread to the Midwest and finally to the east. A major source of anti-Chinese sentiment was organized labor. There was a determined and effective campaign, led by Samuel Gompers of the American Federation of Labor, to force the Chinese out of factory and industrial jobs, and to exclude them completely from the unions.

Local governments enacted punitive and harassing legislation. Chinese were effectively disenfranchised and deprived of all civil rights. They could not testify in court against white people, nor could they own land. Most Chinese women were barred from immigrating to the United States. Between 1890 and 1924, fourteen Chinese-exclusion laws were passed.

Forced out of factory and industrial jobs, the Chinese had virtually disappeared from the labor market by 1910. They retreated and regrouped in the ghettos that became known as Chinatowns, where they were generally restricted to the most menial kinds of labor—laundry work and domestic service—and became largely dependent on the economy of their Chinatown communities.

The miniscule number of Chinese women who were the wives of merchants, and therefore able to join their husbands, were kept in almost total isolation, rarely leaving their homes or Chinatown. One result of the shortage of Chinese women in the community was the growth of prostitution, which continued well into the twentieth century.

American attitudes toward the Chinese have always been a direct reflection of United States foreign policy. Thus, at different times, the Chinese have been perceived as sly and crafty, as honest and loyal, as heathen and immoral, and as wise and scholarly. And all of those images have been reinforced by the mass media. Chinese women have been seen as exotic and sexy or as subservient wives and amahs. Little recognition has been given to the important contributions of Chinese men and women to the development of the United States.

America's alliance with China in World War II fostered a more favorable climate and was a significant factor in the elimination of discriminatory immigration laws. A quota system replaced what was an almost total prohibition of Chinese entry. In 1943, Chinese aliens became eligible for citizenship, and the War Brides Act of 1945 permitted the admission of Chinese wives and fiancées of American servicemen into the United States.

In this period there was a favorable image of the Chinese as filial, industrious, and law-abiding. But soon that friendly attitude was dissipated by the chill in United States–China relations following the 1949 Communist victory in China. The Korean War and later the Vietnam War aroused considerable enmity, which again had negative affects on Chinese Americans.

During all this vacillation, ordinary Chinese Americans continued to experience discrimination on both personal and social levels. They were denied housing in white neighborhoods, passed over for professional positions and advancement, barred from membership in social clubs, and restricted in admission to colleges and universities.

### *Chinatown and the Emergence of a Middle Class*

Aptly dubbed "the gilded ghettos", the Chinatowns of today are densely populated by immigrant working-class people. Since 1965, when rigid quotas were abolished, there has been a tremendous increase in immigration to the United States from Taiwan, Hong Kong, and China. Between 1975 and the end of 1981, about 550,000 Vietnamese refugees, many of them ethnic Chinese, entered the country. A major development has been the dramatic increase in the number of Chinese women im-migrants in the 20- to 50-year-old age bracket.

The majority of immigrants settle first in the Chinatowns of the major coastal cities of the eastern and western United States, straining the resources of those areas to the breaking point. New York's Chinatown, for example, is now the largest Chinese community outside Asia.

There is a growing Chinese American middle class composed of college-educated second and third generations, and of immigrant students, scientists, and scholars. However, integration into the middle class has not been smooth, since economic success is not always accompanied by complete social acceptance. Many Chinese Americans have moved into formerly white neighborhoods and suburbs, but they have had to overcome discriminatory real estate practices. In the workplace, many professionals encounter subtle forms of discrimination, which makes advancement difficult or impossible. In the skilled crafts, determined opposition to Chinese American membership from organized labor is more blatant.

The relative gains made by some middle- and working-class Chinese Americans have led to the myth that they are a successful "model minority" that has "made it" in business and the professions. The stereotype belies the grim realities of juvenile delinquency, poverty, educational deficiencies, employment problems, and physical and mental illness that exist in Chinatowns.

### *Chinese Americans and Mental Illness*

Child-rearing practices in Chinese families emphasize strict parental control. Children are taught to submit to the authority of parents, older relatives, and community leaders. Great importance is attached to educational achievement, obedience, conformity, and correct social behavior. A strong, sometimes oppressive, sense of responsibility to the family is instilled. Female children especially are often overprotected and taught to be self-effacing and deferential.

Trouble arises when these cultural values clash with the individualistic values of the dominant society. Assertiveness and the drive for self-fulfillment result in conflict with parents, often producing intense guilt and alienation.

A study by Berk and Hirata (1973) disputes the popular stereotypical notion that Chinese Americans have no serious mental health problems. Since the 1930s both male and female Chinese Americans have shown a marked increase in their rate of commitment to mental institutions; it is roughly equal to that of the general population. Before the 1930s, the rate of commitment for Chinese Americans was substantially lower. Moreover, there is evidence that those Chinese Americans who are committed to mental institutions are more severely disturbed than white patients.

Lyman (1974) reports a disturbingly high rate of suicide among Chinese American women, rising from 17.5 percent in the 1950s to 28.3 percent in the 1960s. The methods these women chose for ending their lives—hanging, poisoning, and jumping from high buildings—were tragically indicative of their isolation. Many Chinese Americans, although not disturbed enough to be diagnosed as mentally ill, experience feelings of frustration and alienation resulting from both covert and overt manifestations of racism.

A comprehensive study by Sue and Kirk (1975), psychologists at the University of California at Berkeley, reveals that Chinese American students are markedly more inhibited and socially withdrawn than the general student norm. Another study, by Fong and Peskin (1973), found that Chinese American females scored lower than non-Chinese students on "socialization and good impression" as a measure of conflict with sex-role expectations.

Sue identifies three distinct modes of personality accommodation:

1. The *traditionalist* has internalized the cultural heritage of Confucian precepts, and socializes almost exclusively with the subculture.
2. The *marginal person* suffers from an identity crisis, defining self-worth in terms of acceptance by Caucasians and denial of the minority culture. The result is often alienation from the subculture but less than full acceptance by the dominant society.

3. The *Asian American* is in the process of forging a new identity: retaining pride in the cultural heritage while loosening the parental hold. The new Asian American woman refuses to limit her personal growth, and strives actively to combat racism and to change society for the better. In this effort, she must struggle against both the Asian and the western concepts of femininity. The Asian American woman derives pride from raising group esteem and from involvement in community programs to provide health care, recreational services, and educational reforms. Yet the Asian American woman finds that her emerging role is not fully accepted by all segments of her own society, as Asian American men continue to deny her equality in an effort to prove their own masculinity.

***Employment Status: Concerns and Needs***

Chinese American women are a hardworking lot, participating in the labor force in greater proportion than other women. The 1970 census shows that 50 percent of all Chinese American women were employed, compared with 41 percent of white women. More recent statistics show an employment rate above 60 percent. It should also be noted that these statistics do not take into account the large numbers of unpaid female workers in small family businesses such as restaurants, grocery stores, and curio shops.

Many Chinese American women are postponing marriage, and tend to have families smaller than the average. It is clear that Chinese American women work out of economic necessity; Chinese American men experience job discrimination, which limits their earning power and makes it essential for many wives to work. More than 60 percent of Chinese American families have two or more wage earners, whereas only 51 percent of families in the majority population have more than one. In 1975, 17 percent of Chinese American families had incomes below the poverty level, compared with 9 percent of families in the majority population.

A striking characteristic of the employment pattern of Chinese women is the phenomenon of occupational segregation--concentration in a small range of occupations. More than half of all employed United States-born Chinese women are low-status, white-collar workers in such positions as typist, secretary, office clerk, and salesperson. More than half of all foreign-born Chinese women are employed as factory workers, domestic helpers, and service workers. Fewer than 3 out of 100 hold the high-paying craft jobs.

Chinese American women are underrepresented in high-visibility fields such as the mass media and the creative and performing arts. Although 19.4 percent of Chinese American women hold professional jobs, they tend to be concentrated in the lower ranks. For example, they are more likely to be accountants, nurses, and health technicians than lawyers, doctors, and engineers. Only 3.8 percent are in the managerial-administrative category.

A considerable proportion of Chinese American women have attained high levels of education. However, their wages are not commensurate with their training. In 1970, 9.3 percent of college-educated Chinese American women earned $10,000, compared with 59.6 percent of white male college graduates and 38.3 percent of Chinese American male college graduates.

One area in which Chinese American women are conspicuously underemployed is the Federal Civil Service. A Civil Service Commission study found that the median grade level of Asian American women was below that of both white women and black women, even though a much higher percentage of Asian American women had college degrees.

Another disturbing instance of the underutilization of Chinese Americans is the difficulties faced by recent immigrants who were highly trained professionals in the countries from which they came. Because of rigid licensing rules and regulations, noncitizen status, and lack of fluency in English, many such persons have not been able to secure work commensurate with their ability and experience. Out of economic necessity, they have had to settle for less desirable jobs.

The stereotype of the quiet, agreeable, industrious Chinese woman undoubtedly contributes to these patterns of underemployment and occupational segregation. On the one hand, employers tend to relegate Chinese American women to routine, dead-end jobs; on the other hand, Chinese American women often accept others' views about what types of work and behavior are suitable for them. Racism and sexism are still deeply rooted in the social structure, even in the educated class.

At the lowest rung of the economic ladder are large numbers of older, foreign-born Chinese American women who work in the garment and service industries of Chinatowns. With little education, they work long hours under substandard conditions for pitifully low wages. A study by Fong and Cabezas (1980) reported that the average annual income of these women was $2,000. The oversupply of labor serves to keep wages low. In studying Chinatown sweatshops, Lan (1976) found that, compared with the pay received by those in other industries, garment workers' wages have actually declined. The existing unions have been notoriously unresponsive to the needs and problems of Chinese American women.

In 1970, 22.5 percent of all Chinese American women were employed in the garment industry. In San Francisco, the figure was 31 percent; in New York, 46 percent of the city's Chinese American women were employed by the garment industry as sewing machine operators. These women commonly work long hours under substandard conditions. Even though 72 percent have husbands who also work, their combined income, as of 1970, was still below the poverty level.

Sewing in the sweatshops is often the only kind of work open to Chinese American women. Fearful of losing their jobs, they endure oppressive conditions and exploitation. Too timid to protest and having no other work opportunities, they are effectively trapped. Often they carry the double burden of household responsibilities and outside employment. Many have young children, which often adds to their problems because of the lack of day care centers.

Unfamiliar with governmental agencies and institutions, and limited in their ability to speak English, many Chinese American families are unaware of the social services and welfare benefits to which they are entitled. Even those who do receive some Social Security and welfare benefits receive substantially less assistance than other families. In New York, for instance, Chinese American families receive $626 less than the average family of the same size receiving benefits. Such inequities result in needless suffering and a tragic waste of human resources.

***Educational Status***

Chinese American women are concentrated at each end of the educational ladder. At the top are the 17 percent who have graduated from college. However, their employment status does not reflect their level of educational attainment. At the bottom of the ladder are about 24 percent who have had seven or fewer years of school. In the core areas of Chinatown, the level of educational attainment is even lower.

Yet educational equity cannot be measured simply in quantitative terms, that is, in number of years of formal schooling. It does not necessarily follow that additional years of education automatically lead to occupational advancement. When statistics show that Chinese American females earn only 42 percent of the average annual salary of white males having a comparable education, one must ask whether there are factors in the educational process itself that affect the attainment of true equity.

It seems apparent that the education Chinese American women receive does not adequately prepare them for the competitive job market. It also seems apparent that our educational system does not meet the needs of those who could profit the most from vocational training, those who because of cultural, linguistic, and institutional barriers cannot take advantage of training that is available in the dominant society.

### *Problems with Stereotypes and Cultural Pressures*

That institutional practices do influence academic and vocational choices is obvious. The evidence suggests that there are subtle pressures that channel Chinese American students into scientific and technical fields in which a minimum of self-expression is required, and in which the opportunities for moving into managerial or policymaking positions are few. In these fields, the level of aspiration is likely to be set lower. For example, a Chinese American woman might choose to be a pharmacist rather than a physician.

For some Chinese American students, high expectations from teachers and heavy pressures from family to excel may produce an overwhelming fear of failure. The relentless pursuit of good grades tends to inhibit social activity and to discourage creativity and personal development. The intellectual and emotional isolation of many Chinese American students has been observed by several psychologists.

Counselors often unconsciously steer pupils down vocational and academic paths that *they* think are suitable for them, instead of basing recommendations on pupils' true interests and aptitudes. Chinese American women, in particular, are constantly encountering limitations imposed on their ambitions by the supposed superiority of men and the family view of what is suitable work and behavior for women.

There is an urgent need to explore new alternatives for Chinese American women, to design new programs, to fill the gaps in their education, and to provide support services while these women experiment with nontraditional career options.

### *Language Problems and Cultural Education*

One of the major difficulties that hamper the Chinese American student is English language deficiency. Chinese remains the language spoken at home by 96 percent of foreign-born children and 70 percent of the second generation—astonishing rates. Since these students have far less exposure to middle- and upper-class spoken English, it is hardly surprising to find that as a group they score significantly lower on verbal skills tests and are less articulate in class and in situations in which speaking ability is especially important. Not surprising, then, is that Chinese American students tend to enter disciplines requiring quantitative skills but a minimum of self-expression (for example, engineering). They are greatly underrepresented in the humanities, the arts, and the social sciences. In addition, role models in public office, the media, and the performing arts are scarce, in part because the ethnic culture discourages spontaneity and outspokenness.

The failure to incorporate into school curricula full recognition of Chinese contributions to American society, the misunderstanding of the historical relationship between China and the United States, and the absence of meaningful cross-cultural interaction do little to enhance ethnic self-esteem and self-confidence. Consider the plight of the younger immigrant who is thrust into an insensitive and unresponsive school situation in which the curriculum is devoid of anything to induce pride in the individual's own history or culture.

### *Recommendations*

Most Chinese American women share the same problems of underemployment and occupational segregation, though at sharply different levels. Those with higher levels of education, no less than those with limited schooling, have an urgent need for continuing education to enable them to make the most of their talents and to achieve fulfillment in satisfying, challenging work. They also have a need for equal opportunities in the workplace and for equal pay for equal work.

Following are some general recommendations to achieve these goals.

1. Sensitivity training for guidance counselors to make them aware of the special needs of Chinese American women who are about to enter the labor force. Career counseling should inform and encourage Chinese American women to look beyond the "safe" occupations.
2. Bilingual, cross-cultural education in basic rights; information about health, social, and legal services in the community.
3. Vocationally oriented English language training; job training to upgrade and expand employment opportunities for the underemployed.
4. Continuing education to promote upward mobility and the establishment of a network to recruit Chinese American women for administrative positions and nonstereotyped professions. Such programs might include instruction in job search techniques, assertiveness training, and psychological counseling to offset cultural pressures.

5. Publicizing of role-models—Chinese American women who have made extraordinary achievements in spite of obstacles.
6. Dissemination of cultural information to counteract the Hollywood stereotypes of exotic dragon ladies or docile servant girls.

***Summary***

The Chinese American woman bears the double burden of racism and sexism. She must often contend with demeaning stereotypes of Chinese women. Frequently, she is at odds with herself and with others when deeply ingrained cultural traits of deference and reserve conflict with her own aspirations to develop and utilize her talents to the fullest.

Although some Chinese American women attain high levels of education, their job status is not consistent with their training. There is a clear pattern of being confined to low-paying clerical, service, or operative work; of experiencing restrictions in upward mobility; and of contending generally with inferior employment status and benefits.

Foreign-trained professionals are confronted with rigid licensing practices by professional organizations and state legislatures in the United States, which makes it difficult, if not impossible, for them to find suitable employment.

Chinese American women are conspicuously absent from occupations having an impact on public policy and from administrative and managerial positions.

More than half of the foreign-born Chinese American women are in low-level, blue collar jobs, notably in the garment and food service industries, where the pay is low and the hours long. With little or no education, poor language skills, and the barriers of racial and sex-role stereotyping, these women have no other job opportunities available to them. Moreover, they must work to ensure the survival of their families.

Chinese American women work in significantly greater proportion than other women do, but they earn less on the average. There is a strong sense of frustration and a lack of fulfillment arising from their inability to achieve employment commensurate with their training, or to gain access to opportunities to upgrade job skills.

Chinese American women need to develop leadership, a group identity, and a support system to encourage one another.

Since the repeal of the immigration exclusion laws in 1965, there has been a dramatic increase in the number of female Chinese Americans entering this country. Statistics show that more than 50 percent of the present Chinese American population has only recently arrived in the United States.

It is clear that if Chinese American women are to achieve educational and occupational equity, new and imaginative programs must be developed. There should be training to overcome cultural conditioning; career counseling to encourage entry into nontraditional jobs; and bilingual, vocationally oriented programs to enable those with inadequate English language ability to break out of the sweatshops and kitchens of Chinatown, to upgrade their job skills, and to expand their horizons.

***References***

Berk, Bernard B., and Lucie Cheng Hirata. "Mental Illness among the Chinese: Myth or Reality?" *Journal of Social Issues* 29, no. 2 (1973): 149-66.

Commission on Civil Rights. *Civil Rights Issues of Asian and Pacific Americans: Myths and Realities*. Washington, D.C.: Commission on Civil Rights, 1979.

Equal Employment Opportunity Commission. *Equal Employment Opportunity Report, 1973: Job Patterns for Minorities and Women in Private Industry*. Washington, D.C.: The Commission, 1975.

Fong, Pauline L., and Amado Y. Cabezas. "Economic and Employment Status of Asian Pacific Women." Conference on the Educational and Occupational Needs of Asian-Pacific American Women. Washington, D.C.: National Institute of Education, Department of Education, 1980.

Fong, Stanley L.M., and Harvey Peskin. "Sex-Role Strain and Personality Adjustment of China-Born Students in America: A Pilot Study." In *Asian American Psychological Perspectives*, edited by Stanley Sue and Nathaniel N. Wagner, 79-85. Palo Alto, Calif.: Science and Behavior Books, 1973.

Lan, Dean. "Chinatown Sweatshops." In *Counterpoint: Perspectives on Asian America*, edited by Emma Gee, 347-58. Los Angeles: Asian American Studies Center, University of California Press, 1976.

Lott, Juanita Tamayo, and Canta Pian. *Beyond Stereotypes and Statistics: Emergence of Asian and Pacific American Women*. Washington, D.C.: Organization of Pan Asian American Women, Inc., 1979.

Lyman, Stanford. *Chinese Americans*. New York: Random House, 1974.

———. *Social Indicators of Equality for Minorities and Women*. Washington, D.C.: Commission on Civil Rights, 1978.

Sue, Derald W., and Barbara A. Kirk. "Asian-Americans: Use of Counseling and Psychiatric Services on a College Campus." *Journal of Counseling Psychology* 20, no. 1 (1975): 84-86.

Sue, Stanley, and Derald Wing Sue, "Chinese American Personality and Mental Health." *Amerasia Journal* 1 (1971): 36-49.

U.S. Department of Commerce, Bureau of the Census. *Subject Report: Japanese, Chinese and Filipinos in the United States*, 1970 Census of Population. Washington, D.C.: Government Printing Office, 1980.

U.S. Department of Health, Education and Welfare. *A Study of Selected Socioeconomic Characteristics of Ethnic Minorities Based on the 1970 Census*. Vol. 2: *Asian Americans*. Washington, D.C.: U.S. Department of Health, Education and Welfare, Office of Special Concerns, HEW Publication no. 05 (1974): 75-121.

## Chinese American Women: A Select Bibliography

***Introduction***

This bibliography has been compiled to cover many aspects of the life of Chinese American women, with particular reference to educational and employment equity. While we were conducting a literature search on Chinese American women as part of our project, we found that we needed to sift through a lot of peripheral materials to reach what was relevant. In addition, individual researchers and institutions have consistently expressed the need for a comprehensive bibliography on Chinese American women. Therefore, we decided to record, maintain, and expand a file of all relevant references. The result is this select bibliography.

The bibliography can be used by researchers, community workers, policymakers—all those who are concerned about, and wish to contribute their efforts to, the welfare of Chinese American women. These users will find the bibliography helpful in facilitating their search for information and data. By compiling this bibliography, we hope to contribute our knowledge and efforts to educational and employment equity for Chinese American women, and eventually for all minority women.

***Scope***

Chinese American women are defined as ethnic Chinese women who are American citizens, either by birth or by naturalization, or who are permanent residents. The primary selections are materials on Chinese American women. However, other references that deal with Chinese Americans in general and with Asian American women are also included.

***Classification Scheme of the Bibliography***

Entries are divided into six different categories designed for both general use and scholarly research. We have included some audiovisual materials, such as slides and films, as well as print resources. Those books and journal articles that are published in Chinese have been flagged with an asterisk.

Following is a general description of the six categories into which the bibliography is organized.

1. *Historical References* includes materials relevant to the historical experience of the Chinese immigrant. It also deals with the development of various Chinese communities.

2. *Education and Employment* includes various issues dealing with employment and education, as well as other fields concerned with teaching and learning, such as education, employment, and economic status; educational leadership; alternatives in education and employment; racial and ethnic employment patterns; working life and conditions; workforce and socioeconomic characteristics; earning gaps; educational and occupational needs; teaching methods; and classroom responses.
3. *Social-Psychological Studies* includes research on mental processes and behavior, and behavioral characteristics of an individual and/or group in the social context, such as acculturation, adjustment, and integration; mental ability; changing attitudes; language development; self-concept and socialization; cultural conflict; personality adjustment; and mental illness.
4. *Literature and Other Resources* includes prose or verse (fiction, plays, essays, poems, etc.). Biographical sketches and essays on the mood of a time are also included. (It should be noted that we have not done extensive research in this category. Additional citations in this area can be found in other resources.)
5. *Other Social Issues and Problems* includes various issues and concerns other than those listed above, such as juvenile delinquency, politics, the women's movement, family and children, community problems, racism, aging, health, stereotypes, immigration, feminism, and sexism.
6. *General References* includes general information on social and cultural background, studies on Chinese women in Asia, and studies on Chinese Americans in the United States.

***Source of References***

References for the bibliography came from the following sources:

- American University, Computer Search
- *Annotated Bibliography on Asian Women*
- Asian American Mental Health Resource Center, Bibliography on Pacific/Asians in American Immigration
- *Bilingual Education Bibliographical Abstracts*
- Bureau of the Census, U.S. Department of Commerce
- *Dissertation Abstracts*
- ERIC: Data Base Name
- Library of Congress

- National Association for Asian and Pacific American Education
- National Clearinghouse on Mental Health, National Institute on Mental Health
- *Psychological Abstracts*
- Smithsonian Science Information Exchange
- *Sociological Abstracts*
- Women's Educational Equity Communications Network, *Resource Roundup: Asian/Pacific Women in America*

# APPENDIX 2

## "CHINESE AMERICAN WOMEN ORGANIZE"

*Editor's note:* Copied from the *Congressional Record* 125:28 (March 8, 1979): E 1014–1015.

CHINESE AMERICAN WOMEN ORGANIZE

---------------

HON. PAUL SIMON

OF ILLINOIS

IN THE HOUSE OF REPRESENTATIVES

*Thursday, March 8, 1979*

• Mr. SIMON Mr. Speaker, recently I had the privilege of meeting Pauline W. Tsui, president of the recently established Organization of Chinese American Women.

She gave me a paper called "Problems and Issues Facing Chinese American Women.' I found three things of particular interest in their statement. One is that according to the" 1970 census, 48 percent of all Chinese women worked in 1970 while only 13 percent did in 1960.

Second, 17 percent of Chinese American women are college graduates. More than twice the proportion of women in the total U.S. population, which is 8 percent.

Third, Chinese women are underemployed in the Federal civil service.

I am inserting the statement in the RECORD for my colleagues who I believe will find their statement of interest, and for the Federal employing agencies who can help to rectify the imbalance in employment.

The statement follows:

PROBLEMS ANO ISSUES FACING CHINESE AMERICAN WOMEN

Chinese American women face a variety of problems and issues. Some of these are uniquely our own; others we share with all Asian American women; all minority women; and all American women.

Chinese American women are characterized first and foremost by our diversity. We differ in where we were born, in how long we have been in America, and in what languages and dialects we speak. Our life styles, education and socio-economic backgrounds are as different as night and day depending on whether we live in the ghettos of Chinatown or in the suburbs. Among our ranks are found doctors as well as sweat shop workers, teachers as well as housekeepers. The aggregate census statistics do not and cannot tell our whole story.

Chinese American women are a hard working lot. We work proportionately in greater numbers than other women in helping to support our families. Between 1960 and 1970, the labor force participation rate of Chinese women increased to 50 percent from 44 percent, with the greatest increase occurring among married women. Forty-eight percent of all Chinese wives worked in 1970 when only 13 percent did in 1960.[1] For them as for all women, equal access to employment opportunities is a major concern;

Education is another important part of our story. The educational attainment of some Chinese American women is very high. Seventeen percent are college graduates— more than twice as many proportionally as for women in the total U.S. population (8%).[2] When presented with such statistics, it is surprising that underemployment is a major problem for Chinese American women who are college-educated. In the total U.S. population, the ratio of women who are college graduates to those who are employed in professional and managerial positions is 1 to 1. For the Chinese women, however, the proportion is only 1. 0.7.[3] The differential, it would appear, reflects that many Chinese American women have not been hired at levels commensurate with their training.

One of the areas in which Chinese American women are underemployed is in Federal Service. Findings from a Civil Service Commission study confirmed that Asian American women who are working in the U.S. government had the highest educational levels among women of all groups (21% were college graduates compared to 11% of white women in the U.S. government). The median grade levels of Asian American women with college trainings however, was lower than the median grade levels of both white and black women with college training.[4]

Chinese women as a whole are conspicuous in our absence from administrative, managerial and policy-making positions, like our male counter-parts, Chinese American women professionals concentrate in technical fields, namely health and science. We are sorely lacking in many important professions that have major impact on public policy including; public administration, law, journalism, finance and international relations. Unlike other women, we are even hard to find in the social services area.

Currently, Chinese women both in America are concentrated in two job categories: clerical and sales. More than half of the working U.S. born Chinese women are employed in clerical and other low-level white collar jobs. Again, underemployment is an important factor.

Most foreign born Chinese women tend to have a different set of employment problems. While the median schooling of Chinese American women is 12.5 years, many Chinese women living in Chinatowns have never had as much opportunity to be educated. In San Francisco and New York City, cities with the largest Chinatowns in America, the median schooling of Chinese women is less than 10 years.[5] The foreign born, many of whom are recent immigrants, generally lack English language skills and often lack relevant education. Over half (64%) of all foreign born Chinese women are working in low level blue collar jobs.[6] Typically, these women are relegated to working long hours for meager wages in garment factories or Chinese restaurants.

Older Chinese American women are likely to suffer even more, serious problems. Like all Asian elderly, older Chinese American women often do not receive social services because of language, racial and cultural barriers. Health and welfare agencies have few bilingual staff and very little outreach is made to the Chinese communities about their services. Older Chinese American women are particularly poorly informed about the availability of services and fail to use existing programs to which they are entitled because of language handicaps and cultural inhibitions.

Chinese women share many common problems with other women. Where work is in- {Footnotes at end of article.} volved we find it difficult to break out of traditional female occupations. Too often we face the dual roles of housewife and worker without the necessary support services such as child care, household help or the sharing of duties at home. Most of us are relegated to low-paying and low status jobs without access to upward mobility.

Our problems are compounded by racial discrimination, prejudice and stereotypes. In addition, we are further bound by traditions and norms that treasure boys and undervalue girls. From infancy, Chinese girls are taught to cater to the needs and wishes of the men in their lives—father, husband and son. We must learn to deal with cultural inhibitions against self expression and assertiveness.

Chinese American women must step lightly between the confining stereotypes of the, "model minority" and the exploitative stereotype projected in the media. While other women need to break out from traditional female occupations, Chinese American women must first overcome the images so often draw in fiction that we are "Dragon Ladies," submissive servant girls, or exotic ladies of the night.

Fundamentally, Chinese American woman need to achieve legal and economic equality with men, equal pay for work of equal value, equal access to credit and equal opportunities to participate in the power structure.

Overall Chinese American women must forge a consciousness and a group identity. We need access to assertiveness and leadership training, means to improve our communication skills and greater visibility and representation in the political arena. Future goals must also include greater opportunities to participate in decision making forums.

NOTES

[1] U.S. DHEW, Office of Special Concerns, *A Study of Selected Socioeconomic Characteristics of Ethnic Minorities Based on the 1970 Census,* Volume II Asian Americans, (1974).

[2] *Ibid.*

[3] *Ibid.*

[4] *Civil Rights Digest,* Volume 9, Number 1, Fall, 1976).

[5] *Op. cit.*, U.S. DHEW.

[6] *Ibid.*

# Appendix 3
## Asian/Pacific-American Heritage Month

*Editor's note:* From *Congressional Record* 138:141 (October 4, 1992): H 11278–11281.

Mr. SAWYER. Mr. Speaker, I move to suspend the rules and pass the bill (H.R. 5572) to designate May of each year as 'Asian/Pacific-American Heritage Month.'

The Clerk read as follows:

**H.R. 5572**

Be it enacted by the Senate and House of Representatives of the United States of America in Congress assembled,

SECTION 1. CONGRESSIONAL FINDINGS.

The Congress finds that--

(1) on May 7, 1843, the 1st Japanese immigrants came to the United States;

(2) on May 10, 1869, Golden Spike Day, the 1st transcontinental railroad in the United States was completed with significant contributions from Chinese pioneers;

(3) in 1979, at Congress' direction, the President proclaimed the week beginning on May 4, 1979, as Asia/Pacific American Heritage Week, providing an opportunity for the people of the United States to recognize the history, concerns, contributions, and achievements of Asian and Pacific Americans;

(4) in 1990, 1991 and 1992, Congress designated and the President proclaimed the month of May as Asian/Pacific American Heritage Month;

(5) nearly 8,000,000 people in the United States can trace their roots to Asia and the islands of the Pacific; and

(6) Asian and Pacific Americans have contributed significantly to the development of the arts, sciences, government, military, commerce, and education in the United States.

SEC. 2. ANNUAL COMMEMORATION.

(a) **Designation:** May of each year is designated as 'Asian/Pacific American Heritage Month'.

(b) **Federal Proclamation:** The President is authorized and requested to issue annually a proclamation calling on the people of the United States to observe the month designated in subsection (a) with appropriate programs, ceremonies and activities.

(c) **State Proclamations:** The chief executive officer of each State is requested to issue annually a proclamation calling on the people of the State to observe the month designated in subsection (a) with appropriate programs, ceremonies and activities.

(d) **Definition:** For purposes of subsection (c), the term 'State' means any of the several States, the District of Columbia, the Virgin Islands of the United States, the Commonwealth of Puerto Rico, Guam, American Samoa, the Commonwealth of the Northern Mariana Islands, the Republic of the Marshall Islands, the Federated States of Micronesia, and Palau.

The SPEAKER pro tempore. Pursuant to the rule, the gentleman from Ohio [Mr. **Sawyer**] will be recognized for 20 minutes, and the gentleman from New York [Mr. **Horton**] will be recognized for 20 minutes.

The Chair recognizes the gentleman from Ohio [Mr. **Sawyer**].

Mr. SAWYER. Mr. Speaker, I yield myself such time as I may consume.

Mr. Speaker, I am pleased to bring before the House legislation to designate May of each year as 'Asian/Pacific-American Heritage Month'.

H.R. 5572 is the product of many years of work by the distinguished dean of the New York delegation, **Frank Horton.** Congressman **Horton** is retiring at the end of this Congress, after 30 years of service in this body.

So, first, I want to use this opportunity to extend my best wishes to Frank and his family, and to recognize his enormous contributions to this institution and to the American people.

**Frank,** we are grateful for your leadership and guidance over these many years. You have consistently placed principle and fairness over partisan concerns. You have been a conciliator in the true sense of the word. Your skills as a legislator will be missed.

Mr. Speaker, H.R. 5572 would designate an annual public observance in recognition of the fastest growing segment of our population, Asian-Americans.

Since 1978, when Congress first considered legislation to recognize the contributions of Asian-Americans, the number of Americans of Asian and Pacific Islander heritage has more than doubled, to nearly 8 million.

This population is also enormously diverse, with many ethnic backgrounds of differing language and culture. Some Asian groups have been in the United States for several generations; others are more recent immigrants.

The longstanding policy of the Committee on Post Office and Civil Service governing commemorative legislation prohibits recurring annual commemoratives. Over the years, the committee has diligently enforced that provision of the policy.

However, in a few instances, and after careful review beyond our usual standard for commemoratives, the committee has approved exceptions to the policy.

Those exceptions were granted in cases where the committee determined that the subject matter was of extraordinary national significance and where circumstances clearly supported a waiver from the stated policy.

Applying that strict standard, the committee found a clear basis for approving an exception to the policy for H.R. 5572.

The subject matter of the bill is of extraordinary national significance in light of the substantial demographic change sweeping the country. The United States truly continues to be a nation of immigrants, and the diversity of the population continues to contribute to the strength and progress of the Nation.

The committee also considered the existence of similar annual periods of public observance in recognition of other numerically large racial minority groups.

In 1968, Congress enacted legislation designating 'National Hispanic Heritage Week.' That act was later amended to extend the recognition to a month, from September 15 to October 15 of each year.

In addition, the President annually designates February as 'Black History Month.'

Accordingly, Mr. Speaker, I urge my colleagues to support this effort by the gentleman from New York.

Mr. Speaker, I reserve the balance of my time.

[Page: H11279]

Mr. HORTON. Mr. Speaker, I yield myself 8 minutes.

Mr. Speaker, I am honored to be the primary sponsor of H.R. 5572. As the gentleman from Ohio [Mr. **Sawyer**] explained, this bill would designate the month of May of each year as Asian/Pacific American Heritage Month.

In addition to the annual designation of the month, my legislation would request that the President and the Governor of each State annually issue a proclamation calling on the people of the United States to observe the month designated with appropriate programs, ceremonies and activities.

I want to thank the chairman, and the ranking minority member of the Post Office and Civil Service Committee, Mr. **Clay** and Mr. **Gilman,** for their strong support for my legislation to designate May of each year as Asian/Pacific American Heritage Month. I also want to express my appreciation to the chairman of the Subcommittee on Census and Population, Representative **Tom Sawyer** of

Ohio, and also the ranking minority member of the subcommittee, Representative **Tom Ridge** of Pennsylvania, for their assistance in bringing this measure to the floor in an expedited fashion.

On June 30, 1977, I had the unique honor and pleasure of introducing House Joint Resolution 540 and later House Joint Resolution 1007 which for the first time in this Nation's history, asked the Congress and the people of the United States to set aside a period in May as Asian/Pacific American Heritage Week. I should add that I feel a great deal of satisfaction in the dramatic growth of organizations dedicated to attracting attention to the problems and issues confronting Asian-Americans. Virtually all of these organizations have been formed as a result of the original legislation in 1977.

Asian-Americans are now the fastest growing minority group in America. Nearly 8 million Americans can trace their roots to Asia and the islands of the Pacific.

I am joined in this action by my distinguished colleague from California, Mr. **Norman Mineta,** who was also the original sponsor with me in 1977. Mr. **Mineta** has been one of the strongest supporters in my effort to achieve recognition for Asian/Pacific Americans. Joining with us in support of this measure are Mr. **Matsui** of California, Mr. **Faleomavaega** of American Samoa, Ms. **Molinari** of New York, Mrs. **Mink** of Hawaii, Mr. **Blaz** of Guam, and Mr. **Abercrombie** of Hawaii.

More than 15 years ago a woman came to my office and told my administrative assistant, Ruby Moy, and me a very compelling and

persuasive story. Today, I would like to share the origin of this landmark legislation.

The celebration of Asian-Pacific American Heritage Month has a very deep and personal meaning for Jeanie Jew and her family. Their story began sometime in the 1800's when a young man, M.Y.Lee left Canton, China to find a better life in America. Mr. Lee was one of the first Chinese pioneers to help build the transcontinental railroad. He later became a prominent California businesman. When the Chinese were having difficulties in Oregon, Mr. Lee traveled to Oregon and was killed during that period of unrest. It was a time of anti-Chinese and anti-Asian sentiment. The revelations about Mr. Lee and the story of Asian Americans led this one woman to believe that not only should Asians understand their own heritage, but that all Americans must know about the contributions and histories of the Asian-Pacific American experience in the United States. Jeanie Jew, the creator of the idea for a heritage month is the granddaughter of M.Y.Lee, the early pioneer.

The original resolution designated the week beginning May 4 as Asian-Pacific American Heritage Week because that week included two significant occasions in the proud history of Asian Americans. May 10, 1809, or Golden Spike Day was the day on which the transcontinental railroad was completed, largely by Chinese-American pioneers. May 7, 1843, marks the date of the first arrival of the Japanese in the United States. Both dates will fittingly be included in Asian-Pacific American Heritage Month.

I want to commend the two women who made this event possible, Ruby Moy and Jeanie Jew. Mrs. Jew turned a personal tragedy in her family history into a positive force.

Asian-Pacific American Heritage Month will now be observed by all Americans. I also want to thank Ruby Moy, my administrative assistant, for her efforts to pass this legislation. She holds the highest professional position to a Member of Congress, and is a second generation Asian-American.

In 1977, Mrs. Jew and Ms. Moy cofunded the congressional Asian-Pacific staff caucus, an organization which collectively worked for the establishment of the first heritage proclamation and supports yearly efforts to perpetuate its recognition. The caucus, a group of professional staff members of Asian descent, periodically discusses and reviews legislation and issues of concern to Asian-Pacific Americans.

I take a great deal of pride in my involvement with the Asian-American community. Asian and Pacific Americans have contributed significantly to the development of the arts, sciences, government, military, commerce, and education in the United States.

I hope my colleagues will join me in supporting this resolution and in recognizing the history and contributions of Asian-Pacific Americans, particularly during Asian-Pacific American Heritage Month. Immediately following my statement, I am including a letter I recently received from Mrs. Jeanie Jew for insertion in the **Record**.

**Springfield, VA,** *October 4, 1992.*

Hon. Frank Horton,

*U.S. House of Representatives, Washington, DC.*

**Dear Congressman Horton:** I was deeply saddened to learn of your announcement to retire from the U.S. House of Representatives. Your departure is not only a loss for New York State and the Congress, but especially for a community of nearly 8 million people across the United States--the Asian/Pacific American. When the gavel signifies the end of the 102nd Congress, our voices will be silent for a time--out of respect--because a great person, the distinguished gentleman from the 29th Congressional District of New York, is leaving the Chamber. You have been our Champion.

For more than a decade, as the chief sponsor with your colleague, Congressman Norman Y. Mineta of California, you have introduced every bill and resolution establishing Asian/Pacific American Heritage Week and Month. Since its first observance, the celebration in May has become the single most significant event for Asian and Pacific Islanders and all Americans to learn more about our concerns, contributions, achievements and history in the U.S. Your legislative efforts on behalf of Asian Americans will be the benchmark for others to follow. The passage of H.R. 5572 is not only a tribute to the many people and communities directly involved, but particularly to you and the U.S. Congress for effective leadership--and the formal recognition of the Asian/Pacific American role in America's past, present and future.

My special thanks to your office, professional staff members, and especially to Ruby G. Moy, your Chief of Staff and Administrative Assistant, for her outstanding efforts and commitment to this landmark legislation.

Robert joins me in expressing our heartfelt appreciation and in wishing you and Nancy the very best.

Sincerely,

*Jeanie F. Jew.*

[Page: H11280]

[TIME: 2040]

Mr. SAWYER. Mr. Speaker, I yield 2 minutes to the gentleman from Missouri [Mr. **Clay**], chairman of the full Committee on Post Office and Civil Service, without whose leadership this timely consideration would not be possible.

Mr. CLAY. Mr. Speaker, I thank the gentleman for yielding time to me, and I rise in support of this bill, which is sponsored by my good friend and colleague, the gentleman from New York [Mr. **Horton**].

Mr. Speaker, it is a fitting tribute to the gentleman from New York that we pass this measure in recognition of his great efforts in behalf of the Asian Pacific American community.

I would like to take this opportunity to pay special tribute to my friend and respected colleague, the gentleman from New York [Mr. **Horton**].

Several months ago, **Frank** stood in the well of this House and announced that he would not seek reelection, that he would retire at the conclusion of this year after some 30 years in this House.

I, like many of our colleagues, was stunned and saddened by the announcement. The citizens of New York State will lose a great servant. The Chamber will lose a great legislator. The Federal and postal workers will lose a great champion and, of course, the Nation will lose a great statesman.

I will lose not only a comrade on the legislative battlefield but, most of all, I will lose a longtime companion and ally.

During this Congress, Mr. Speaker, we have become almost complacent over the decisions of colleagues to leave this body. I will miss many of them as time goes by. I miss those who have left before us and those who are about to go. I know one man that I will miss. I'll miss the pat of his large hand on my back, followed by the bellow of that Cajun rolling voice and the citation of some obscure baseball stats on heroes past and present. Too many times the American public watches us on TV as we battle in the legislative rhetoric like characters in a show. What they sometimes forget is that we are real live humans with hearts, souls and feelings, just like them.

**Frank,** I'll miss you, but always know that you'll never be forgotten as a great legislator and statesman. I wish you and Nancy all the joy and happiness that God can spare.

Mr. HORTON. Mr. Speaker, I yield myself such time as I may consume.

I want to thank the gentleman from Missouri for his very fine remarks. I have enjoyed working with him and this committee particularly. I have the greatest regard for his leadership and his dedication. He is a very fine Member of Congress, and the people in his district certainly respect him. They have sent him back many, many times.

But more importantly, he is the voice of the Congress in representing the Federal employees. And I think one of the most important pieces of legislation that I have ever sponsored has been the effort that he and I have been engaged in to try to repeal the Hatch Act so that the fellow Americans who work for the Federal Government can be American citizens just like the rest of us. Because today they are not.

And the Clay-Horton bill, to repeal the Hatch Act, is still pending. I do not think it will be acted on in this Congress, but I am going to leave it up to his leadership to see that it gets enacted in the near future.

They are the only class of people in America that do not have the responsibilities that the rest of Americans have. They cannot participate in the political process like everyone else can. And until that Hatch Act, which is over 50 years of age, is repealed, those people are going to continue to be second-class citizens.

I would certainly hope that in the next Congress that that can be attended to. I have enjoyed my work in the House. It is a great institution. I am proud of it. I am proud of the opportunity that I have had to serve here and particularly to serve on the Committee on the Post Office and Civil Service.

Mr. CLAY. Mr. Speaker, will the gentleman yield?

Mr. HORTON. I yield to the gentleman from Missouri.

Mr. CLAY. Mr. Speaker, I certainly appreciate the kind remarks. I can assure the gentleman that if I am reelected in November, one of the first pieces of legislation that will go on the President's desk, hopefully a President who is committed to freeing the Federal employees from the present bondage that they serve under, not being able to participate fully in the political process, will sign the bill.

Mr. HORTON. Win one for the Gipper. That is me.

Mr. SAWYER. Mr. Speaker, I yield 2 minutes to the gentleman from California [Mr. **Mineta**], a leader whose commitment on behalf of the measure before us is unsurpassed on our side of the aisle.

[TIME: 2050]

Mr. MINETA. Mr. Speaker, I thank my very distinguished friend, the gentleman from Ohio, for yielding me this time.

Mr. Speaker, I rise today in strong support of H.R. 5572, legislation to permanently designate the month of May as Asian-Pacific American Heritage Month.

Along with my distinguished friend and colleague from New York, Congressman **Frank Horton**, I am very proud to be a cosponsor of this important legislation. I wish to thank **Frank** for all of his efforts and interest in issues involving the Asian-Pacific American community.

H.R. 5572 will build on the work **Frank** began in 1979, when the Congress first recognized Asian/Pacific American Heritage Week.

In 1988, this was expanded to a month-long observance, and the legislation before us today will make the designation of May as Asian-Pacific American Heritage Month a permanent one.

The observance of Heritage Month each year has become an important celebration for all Americans of Asian and Pacific Islands ancestry. Around the country, community organizations take advantage of the opportunity it presents to educate our fellow Americans about our communities, our contributions, and our history in America.

I am very proud that today the House is recognizing the importance of this annual celebration by bringing H.R. 5572 to the floor, and I urge my colleagues to join me in voting to approve the bill.

As I said earlier, Mr. Speaker, I am proud to be an original cosponsor of H.R. 5572.

But the fact that this legislation is before us today is truly a tribute to the gentleman from New York [Mr. **Horton**].

This is a year in which many of our colleagues have announced their retirements, Mr. Speaker. But I can think of no departure from this House that saddens me more than **Frank Horton**'s.

As an Asian-Pacific American, I can say truthfully that our communities have never had a greater friend in the Congress than **Frank Horton**. Throughout his career in the House, his has been a voice for justice and equality--for us and for all Americans.

It has been a great honor for me to work with **Frank**, his administrative assistant, Ruby Moi, and his former staff member, Jeanie Jew. They have been true friends, and I know my colleagues join me in wishing **Frank** well in his retirement. He will surely be missed in this institution, he will be missed by this gentleman from California and Mr. **Horton** will be especially missed by the Asian-Pacific American community.

Mr. HORTON. Mr. Speaker, I yield myself such time as I may consume.

Mr. Speaker, I want to take this occasion to thank personally the gentleman from California, **Norm Mineta,** not only for his comments here tonight and for the comments that he has made, but for his support for this legislation.

I also want to take this occasion to thank him and congratulate him on his leadership of H.R. 442, which was to correct a terrible injustice that was done during World War II.

As I have said several times on this floor during the course of debate on that particular legislation, I happened to be serving with the U.S. Army in Italy when the 442d, which was composed of Asian-Pacific Americans, and mostly Chinese and Japanese, landed in Italy. I was there and I greeted them. I watched the course of action and watched them in action, and they were one of the most heroic organizations in the U.S. Army. Many of them died, many of them received medals, and that community was one of the most highly decorated units in the U.S. Army during World War II. It was very appropriate that that bill be designated 442.

I want to take this occasion personally to thank the gentleman from California [Mr. **Mineta**] and his efforts there. That, combined with what we are doing here, and what has resulted as a result of this legislation, I think has brought the Asian-Pacific community together. Today they are making even more contributions than they have ever made, and now they are getting the recognition that they should have.

Mr. Speaker, I have no further requests for time, and I yield back the balance of my time.

[Page: H11281]

Mr. SAWYER. Mr. Speaker, I yield myself such time as I may consume.

I do so only to associate myself with the remarks of the gentleman from New York [Mr. **Horton**] with regard to our mutual friend, the gentleman from California [Mr. **Mineta**]. His leadership on a whole range of Asian and Pacific Islander issues has been exemplary, but I want to take a moment to offer personal thanks for his guidance and assistance in the course of the last several years as we have sought to bring about the full enumeration of that community in our country in all of its diversity, recognizing that, as is the case with so many Americans, they are not of one blood by any means, but rather, come to this country bound together with one belief that all of us together comprise a single nation.

On behalf of that leadership and help I offer personal thanks.

Mr. MATSUI. Mr. Speaker, I rise today in strong support of H.R. 5572, a bill which would designate May of each year as 'Asian-Pacific American Heritage Month.' As an original cosponsor of this legislation, I believe it is important that this legislation becomes law so all Americans can recognize the achievements of Asian-Pacific Americans, and can understand and appreciate the role of Asian Americans and Pacific Americans in the our Nation's history as well as in America's future.

Asian-Pacific Americans owe a great deal to the first generation that struggled to make a life for themselves and their families here in the United States. As a relatively recent group of newcomers to this country, we have the blessing of being closer in touch with our roots. Not only can we celebrate our customs and traditions, we can count the generations of our families going back centuries, and also remember the stories of our families' struggles and accomplishments.

Asian-Pacific Americans have a proud, rich, and diverse history. Our antecedents were pioneers who traveled far to improve the lives of themselves and their families, and helped our Nation achieve its greatness. Our pioneer ancestors made innumerable and immeasurable sacrifices to provide an opportunity for their descendants to succeed in schooling and careers.

We should take great pride as a nation in the history of Asian-Pacific Americans. But we must also realize that the mentality that led that generation to survive in America is keeping second, third, and fourth generation Asian-Americans from reaching their full potential. Our parents, grandparents, and great-grandparents had a survivalist mentality: they wanted to succeed, but they did not want to rock the boat. They did not want to draw attention to themselves or cause problems by attempting to reform society. And perhaps they were not in a position at that time to do so.

But times have changed, and the Asian-Pacific American community can make a difference. Each Asian-Pacific American has a responsibility to provide leadership for the community. I exhort Asian-Pacific Americans across this great land to look beyond yourselves and your immediate family, and I urge you to see what you can contribute to this country. Asian-Pacific Americans must overcome our ancestors' survivalist mentality and be aggressive in talking on challenges. Clearly, we are up against many obstacles: language barriers, stereotypes, and anti-Asian bigotry. But Asian-Pacific Americans must overcome their apathy in their community and in politics if we are to be fully united with the mainstream of America.

I applaud the accomplishments of Asian-Pacific Americans in many diverse fields. Asian-Pacific Americans display professionalism, courage, and leadership in such diverse fields as education, athletics, science, engineering, the arts, medicine, the law, and the small business. Asian-Pacific Americans demonstrate daily to the world that we can be leaders in any field. We must continue to strive for excellence: to make ourselves, and our community, be the best. Let there be no doubt that this in turn will help make our country strong. Asian-Pacific Americans have an indomitable spirit to work and build, our future promises to be as rich and accomplished as our past.

Mr. GILMAN. I rise today in strong support of H.R. 5572 and I would like to commend my good friend and colleague from New York, **Frank Horton,** for introducing this legislation. I would also like to take this opportunity to thank the chairman of the House Post Office and Civil Service Committee, my good friend **Bill Clay,** for his expedient handling of this measure. H.R. 5572 would designate the month of May each year as 'Asian-Pacific American Heritage Month.'

Mr. Speaker, the chairman and the ranking member of the subcommittee on Census and Population, **Tom Ridge,** should be complimented for recommending that an exception to committee policy be granted in this Bill's case and for supporting this legislation in full committee.

Asian-Pacific Americans are the fastest growing segment of our country's population. A newly released profile by the Census Bureau estimates the Asian-Pacific American population to be approximately 7 million, or about 3 percent of our Nation's total population. The survey further showed that most Asian-Pacific Americans are concentrated in the western region of the United States with 94 percent living in our metropolitan areas. My own congressional district in New York has seen a large growth in its Asian-Pacific American population. Asian-Pacific Americans have contributed significantly to our country's culture, society, and economy, and have played an important role in the history of our country.

Mr. Speaker, as an original cosponsor of H.R. 5572, I am pleased to join with and again commend the chief sponsor of this legislation, **Frank Horton,** who has championed many worthy causes for the Asian-Pacific American Community.

Accordingly, Mr. Speaker, I urge my colleagues to join me in supporting H.R. 5572, and to congratulate, the gentleman from New York, **Frank Horton** on his upcoming retirement. **Frank Horton** has served with distinction in this body for the past 30 years. He should be commended for his arduous work on behalf of the American Postal worker and other Federal employees, the Federal Government, and indeed all Americans. Mr. Speaker, **Frank Horton**'s presence and counsel in this body will be sorely missed.

Mr. SAWYER. Mr. Speaker, I have no further requests for time, and I yield back the balance of my time.

The SPEAKER pro tempore (Mr. **Ray**). The question is on the motion offered by the gentleman from Ohio [Mr. **Sawyer**] that the House suspend the rules and pass the bill, H.R. 5572.

The question was taken; and (two-thirds having voted in favor thereof) the rules were suspended and the bill was passed.

A motion to reconsider was laid on the table.

Mr. SAWYER. Mr. Speaker, I ask unanimous consent that all Members may have 5 legislative days in which to revise and extend their remarks on the legislation just passed.

The SPEAKER pro tempore. Is there objection to the request of the gentleman from Ohio?

There was no objection.

# Appendix 4

## OCAW National Leaders, 1977–2009

### Pauline W. Tsui, Co-founder and Founding President, 1977-1983

I was born an American citizen in Nanking, China and grew up in Shanghai. My parents were Dr. John Y. Woo, a physician from Honolulu, Hawaii and Mrs. Sarah Kuo Woo, from Shanghai, a piano teacher who studied music at Oberlin College, Ohio for two years, a rarity at her time. My father believed that a good education was necessary for girls to survive in China. So I graduated from McTyeire High School for Girls and its extended music department and from St. John's University, majoring in education, both schools located in Shanghai.

During the Sino-Japanese War, I left Shanghai for Chungking, a provisional capital in the western region of interior China for the purpose of coming to America to further my education. That trip took over three weeks by train, truck, foot, wheel barrow and through the Chin Mountain range which is famous for its seventy-two peaks. In Chungking, I taught music and gave a piano recital to raise funds to build a much needed kindergarten.

V-J Day came just when I received my passport from Washington D.C. So, instead of having to fly over the Himalayan Hump, I flew back to Shanghai in a transport plane and boarded the second ship to come to America.

In 1947, I completed my M.A. degree in music education in a year at Columbia University, New York with plans to return to China to establish music schools to enrich people's lives. However, Civil War broke out in China. After I met and married T.L.Tsui, a Chinese diplomat, I remained in America. We raised a family of two children and decided to stay on in Washington, D.C.

My husband and I began our new careers and I entered the U.S. Army Map Services as a translator. There, I learned what real life was like. Although I worked hard and made many contributions, when down sizing occurred in government, I was bumped off six grades from my position by a man who had no knowledge nor skills required in my work. I also realized that it happened to women and minorities only in my section.

In the seventies, Chinese Americans began to understand the importance of unity in representing ourselves and our concerns and our needs, so I joined others in forming the Organization of Chinese Americans (OCA). I served as chair of its inaugural gala in 1973 and as one of its national vice-presidents from 1976-1978. I also co-founded its Chinese Youth Activity Organization in 1974-1975.

In 1974, the Army Map Service recommended me to receive a citation for National Volunteers Award from Governor George Romney of Michigan, then president of the National Center for Voluntary Actions.

1975 was designated by the United Nations as the International Women's Year (IWY), calling the world's attention to the unequal status and treatment of women. The U.S. Government followed by establishing the position of Federal Women's Program Manager in each agency. I applied to my agency and was selected as the Federal Women's Program Manager of the Defense Mapping Agency Hydrographic/Topographic Center from 1976-1980. I was responsible for over 700 women employees' equal treatment at work and their equal opportunities of career advancements. In 1978, I co-founded the Potomac Palisade Chapter of the Federally Employed Women and in 1979, I founded the Brookmont Learning Tree Child Care Center for the Center's employees.

In 1977, Julia Chang Bloch and I learned about the available government funds for women's training by women's organizations at the State Department's IWY Advisory Committee. So we-co-founded the Organization of Chinese American Women (OCAW). We submitted a proposal to the U.S. Department of Education, Women's Educational Equity Act Program (WEEAP) for a three-year grant on "Chinese American Women Educational Equity Program" and was awarded a sizable grant in 1980.

I retired from government service and devoted full time to OCAW. As project director, I set-up an office with four full time staff and conducted training conferences in Washington, D.C., Houston, Texas, Los Angeles,

California and New York City. I also established OCAW's first four chapters in those cities.

My other continuing community services were as:

- D.C. Delegate-at-large to the National Women's Conference in Houston, Texas in 1977
- Member of the D.C. Commission of Women, 1985-1986
- Chair and member of the D.C. Commission for Asian and Pacific Islanders Affairs, 1986-1989
- Vice-president of Coalition for Minority women in Business, 1986-1988
- Co-founder of the Chinatown Service Center, 1987-1992
- Member of D.C. Mayor's Steering Committee on America 2000, 1991-1992
- Member of the Advisory Council of Adult Continuing & Community Education, D.C. Public Schools, 1991-1993
- Chair of the Board of the U.S./Pacific Business Development Corp., 1991-1998
- Chair of the Advisory Committee of the Chinese Women's League, Washington, D.C. chapter, 1991-2000
- Vice-president of the Sino-American Cultural Society, 1991-1998
- Executive Director and Acting Executive Director of OCAW, 1983-2007, and
- Treasurer of OCAW National board, 1997-2009.

My privilege of serving Chinese American women for more than three decades has provided me the opportunity to gain true friendships with younger generations. I am amazed by the tremendous number of talents in OCAW's membership and inspired by the many outstanding leaders I have worked with. In OCAW, we truly enjoyed working with each other which dispelled the old Chinese saying characterizing the Chinese race as "a tray of loose sand."

The many equalities achieved by women in the last century are now available for young women to set a new direction for a new women's movement which is what I said to Erin, the youngest of my four grandchildren, in our discussion recently. I sincerely wish young women would seize this opportunity to map out a trajectory to reach a world where women and men can live happily equal together.

I have two children, four grandchildren and an adorable great grandson, all living in the metropolitan Washington, D.C. area.

### AMBASSADOR JULIA CHANG BLOCH, CO-FOUNDER AND CHAIR OF THE BOARD, 1982-1989

Ambassador Julia Chang Bloch, the first Asian American to hold such rank in the U.S. history, has had an extensive career in international affairs and government service, beginning as a Peace Corps Volunteer in Sabah, Malaysia in 1964 and culminating as U.S. Ambassador to the Kingdom of Nepal in 1989. From 1981 to 1988, Ambassador Bloch served at the U.S. Agency for International Development as Assistant Administrator for Food for Peace and Voluntary Assistance and as Assistant Administrator for Asia and the Near East, positions appointed by the president and confirmed by the Senate. She also was the Chief Minority Counsel to a Senate Select Committee; a Senate professional staff member; the Deputy Director of the Office of African Affairs at the U.S. Information Agency; a Fellow of the Institute of Politics at Harvard University's Kennedy School of Government and an Associate of the U.S.-Japan Relations Program of the Center for International Affairs at Harvard.

After 25 years in government service, Ambassador Bloch moved to the corporate sector in 1993, becoming Group Executive Vice President at the Bank of America, where she created the Corporate Relations Department, heading the bank's Public Relations, Government Affairs, and Public Policy operations. From 1996 to 1998, Ambassador Bloch moved into philanthropy, serving as President and CEO of the United States-Japan Foundation, a private grant making institution, with $100 million in assets. Beginning in 1998, Ambassador Bloch shifted her focus to China, first becoming Visiting Professor at the Institute for International Relations and Executive Vice Chairman of the American Studies Center at Peking University, and subsequently affiliating with Fudan University in Shanghai, as well as the University of Maryland as Ambassador-in-Residence at the Institute for Global Chinese Affairs.

A native of China who came to the U.S. at age nine, Ambassador Bloch grew up in San Francisco and earned a bachelor's degree in Communications and Public Policy from the University of California, Berkeley, in 1964, and a master's degree in Government and East Asia Regional Studies from Harvard University in 1967. She was awarded an

Honorary Doctorate of Humane Letters from Northeastern University in 1986.

Ambassador Bloch serves on a number of corporate and non-profit boards, including: Asia Institute for Political Economy, the University of HK, the Atlantic Council, Council of American Ambassadors, US Asia Pacific Council, Meridian International Center, World Affairs Council, the Fund for American Studies, and Penn Mutual Insurance Co. She was elected as a Fellow to the National Academy of Public Administration and is on the Expert/Eminent Persons Register of the ASEAN Regional Forum, a member of the Woodrow Wilson Council, as well as Trustee Emeriti of the Asia Society, Honorary Member of the Board of Directors of the Friends Society of the Asian Division, Library of Congress, and Honorary Fellow of the Foreign Policy Association. A member of the Council on Foreign Relations and American Academy of Diplomacy, she also serves on the Edumasters International Advisory Committee and the Editorial Board of Berkshire Publishing Group's Encyclopedia of China.

She has received numerous awards, and her publications include: *Women and Diplomacy, Bonds Across Borders*, UK: Cambridge Scholars Publishing, 2007; *Nepal: End of Shangri-la*, Liberal Democracy Nepal Bulletin, Vol. 1, No. 1, 2005, *America's Love-Hate Relationship with China*, American Forum Journal of the Fudan University Center of American Studies, 2003, *Commercial Diplomacy, Living with China: US-China Relations in the 21st Century*, an American Assembly book, New York: W.W.Norton, 1995, *Japanese Foreign Aid and the Politics of Burden Sharing*, Yen for Development, New York: Council on Foreign Relations, 1991.

### Hon. Lily Lee Chen, National President, 1983-1984

Ms. Chen has long been active in business and economic development. She has led trade delegations and speaks extensively on Pacific Rim trade affairs.

Ms. Chen has a distinguished record of public service. She was the first Chinese American woman mayor of an American city. Under her mayoral watch the city of Monterey Park, California won the prestigious "All American City Award" in 1984.

She is a Certified Instructor on International Trade, California Community College system. Prior to assuming the corporate helm, she was an executive with the Los Angeles County where she directed government operations, programs and grant management and the supervision of a $70 million program with 500 employees.

Her public service includes the following with the State of California: Governor's appointee, California State World Trade Commission 1987-1991; Member, California Senate Select Committee on Long Range Planning 1982-1985; and Member, California State Mortgage Bond Allocation Commission 1982-1985; Governor Gray Davis appointee: Member, California Commission on Aging, 2003-2008.

Her public service with the Federal government include the following: Secretary of Commerce Appointee Industry Policy Advisory Committee (IPAC) 1994-1996; Member of the U.S. Delegation, (Planning Committee) Fourth World Conference on Women, 1997; Secretary of State's Appointee, Member of Board of Governors, East West Center 1998-2003; and Secretary of Defense's Appointee, Advisory Committee on Women in the Services 1995-1998.

Chen is a Founding Board Member, Committee of 100 USA, 1989-present and Organization of Chinese American Women National President, 1983-1984.

### LILY K. LAI, PH.D., NATIONAL PRESIDENT, 1984-1990

Dr. Lai is an innovative and versatile executive with broad-based global business experience. She has opened up new markets in Asia, Europe and North America for Fortune 500 companies, and has completed more than 40 global start-ups, acquisitions, joint ventures, and strategic alliances. She is active in academic, civic and professional organizations.

Dr. Lai is the president of First American Development Corporation. Previously Dr. Lai held various executive positions at AT&T from 1971 to 1987, including Director of Corporate Strategy and Development, responsible for AT&T's global business development activities; and Director of International Public Affairs and Public Relations, responsible for managing AT&T's relationships with all international constituents (employees, governments, partners, trade associations, press, and advertising agencies). She was the Chief Financial and Planning Officer and Vice President of Asia/Pacific Operations at US West International from 1987 to 1989. Dr. Lai headed the Corporate Planning and Development Department at Pitney Bowes from 1989 to 1993.

Dr. Lai served on the Board of Trustees of Montclair State University; the Board of Directors of SpecTran Corporation and each of its subsidiaries, CyberExpress, Inc., Vision 21 International, Inc., Vision 21 Marketing, Inc.; and advisory Board of Directors of Pace University, Rosenbluth International, Oxford Partners, the Organization of Chinese American Women, and the National Association of Asian American Professional Women.

Dr. Lai is an MIT Sloan Fellow and holds a Ph.D. and an M.A. in Economics from the University of Wisconsin – Madison, as well as an M.S. and a B.S. in Agricultural Economics from the University of Kentucky and National Taiwan University, respectively. She has received many awards and made speeches to both professional and civic groups. Her success stories were published in numerous English and Chinese magazines and newspapers. Dr. Lai was born in a tiny farming and fishing village in Taiwan and is married to Dr. Son Lin Lai. They have one son and three grandchildren.

## FAITH LEE BREEN, PH.D., CHAIR OF THE BOARD, 1989-1993 AND NATIONAL PRESIDENT, 2008-2009

Dr. Breen has over fifteen years of teaching experience. She is a full-time Tenured Management Professor. She has also taught at the graduate level with Central Michigan University and is an Adjunct Professor with he University of Maryland University College Graduate School of Management and Technology.

Dr. Breen has both private and public professional experience. She served as the Deputy Executive Director of the Gates Millennium Scholars Program. She has also worked for the White House, The National Governors' Association and as an expert consultant to the Deputy Under Secretary of Management at the U.S Department of Education. She was also President and Founder of Systems Resource Management, Inc., a firm that did consulting with the U.S. Department of Transportations' Federal Aviation Administration.

Dr. Breen has received numerous awards including: The Cathy S. Bernard Chair, 2001-2001; a Certificate of Appreciation from the Secretary of the U.S. Department of Education; and a Fulbright cholarship. She has also received research grants from the National Science Foundation and the U.S. Department of Education. She is the Founder of Millennium Management Lecture Series at Prince George's Community College and the author of articles in that College's Instructional Forum.

Dr. Breen holds a Ph.D. from the University of Maryland in Education Policy, Planning and Administration, an MPA from Harvard's Kennedy School of Government, an MA from the University of Pittsburgh in Economics, and a BA from the University of Maryland in Economics where she graduated Summa Cum Laude. She is a recipient of a National Defense Language Fellowship.

Dr. Breen has been married for over 35 years and has two children, a daughter and son. She also has two granddaughters. Her son is still very available.

## Hon. Nancy Linn Patton, National President, 1991-1993

Ms. Patton was the director of Marketing, Pearson Corp. Transportation Group. She was formerly the Deputy Assistant Secretary for International Economic Policy for East Asia and the Pacific in International Trade Administration at the U.S. Department of Commerce and was a member of OCAW's Advisory Board. Previously, she was an IBM program manager for External and Community Affairs for the Washington Metropolitan Area. In 1980, Ms. Patton was selected by IBM as a Brookings Institute Congressional Fellow to serve in the Office of Speaker of the U.S. House of Representatives. Earlier, she was a manager in IBM public sector marketing programs for the mid-Atlantic region, and as an office systems product specialist. She earned three times consecutively, the annual Golden Circle Award, which is IBM's highest award for marketing achievement. Ms. Patton has served in Washington, D.C. community affairs as chairperson on the Board of Studio Theater, board member of the National Conference of Christians and Jews, Project Northstar, and was a past director of Food & Friends and Food for All Seasons.

### HON. KATHERINE CHANG DRESS, NATIONAL PRESIDENT, 1993-1997

A member of OCAW's Advisory Board, Ms. Dress was manager, Outreach Environmental Justice, Dallas Area Rapid Transit, a Principal of UNIDUS Corporation. Before that, Ms. Dress was a journalist for Radio/Daily Newspaper/CBS News, an entrepreneur, a refugee resettlement expert, and a Deputy Director of a U.S. National political organization. Ms. Dress was the Deputy Assistant Secretary for International and Territorial Affairs, U.S. Dept. of Interior and an appointee to the Minority Business Development Agency, Dept. of Commerce; the Peace Corps and the U.S. Merit System Protection Board. She received numerous awards for excellence in her many capacities and community service including a Certificate of Appreciation from the U.S. Commission of Minority Business Development and a Point of Light Award from the U.S. Government. As manager of Minority and Women-owned Business Programs at Fannie Mae, she earned several awards for the corporation and a national personal award from the magazine, *Minority Business Week USA.* She served for several years on the DOC.SBA MED Week Planning Committee and as its Vice-chairperson in 1994. She speaks five languages fluently: English, Chinese, French, German and Italian.

### JEANIE FONG LEE JEW, NATIONAL PRESIDENT, 1997-2001

Jeanie Fong Lee Jew is currently the elected Chair of the Fairfax County, Virginia, Commission for Women, representing more than ½ million women and girls in the county. She is a nationally recognized speaker and consultant whose expertise and experiences are associated with programs and projects which focus upon the economic, educational, social or political opportunities of groups and communities. She has been a consultant to Federal agencies, the U.S. Congress, universities and to national organizations on matters relating to women and Asian Pacific Americans. She also has had a long history in working with the U.S. Embassies and the international communities in the greater Washington, D.C. area. Ms. Jew was honored in 2011 as 'Lady Fairfax,' saluting Fairfax County Virginia's most outstanding women and community activities.

She is the *Creator* of the National Asian Pacific American Heritage Week/Month which is celebrated annually in May throughout the Nation. Organizations in the private and public sectors observe this landmark commemoration with programs initiated by Ms. Jew – especially in the areas of education, public and political affairs, and the arts. This Congressional legislation and Public Law are based on her family's life and experiences in the United States. Through the efforts of Jack Herrity, then Chairman of the Fairfax County Board of Supervisors, Fairfax became the First County and government entity to proclaim and acknowledge the Chinese and Asian contributions to America. As a member of the Board of Directors of Virginia Public Television Fairfax and Richmond, she developed a television series of "Heritage Minutes" profiling a history of outstanding APA individuals and events which was presented throughout major markets in the U.S. Asian Americans and Pacific Islanders were never fully acknowledged until Jeanie Jew wrote a proclamation that changed history.

Ms. Jew served as an advisory member to an education scholarship committee funded by the Bill and Melinda Gates Foundation, and was a principal speaker at its leadership conference for young people. The McDonald Corporation selected her to be the "face" of its first I Am Asian/APA Heritage Month website. Involved in the formation of three financial institutions, she was a founder and Vice Chairman of the Board of Virginia's first women's and minority savings bank in McLean, Virginia. Ms. Jew has also served as a member of the Executive Steering Committee of the National Council of Women's Organization (NCWO). She was a speaker at the National Association for Commissions for Women (NACW) 2011 Conference on issues affecting cities and counties, and had one of the largest audience participation in the conference.

## HON. RUBY G. MOY, NATIONAL PRESIDENT, 2001-2002

The Honorable Ruby G. Moy is currently President and CEO of the Asian American & Pacific Islander American Association of Colleges and Universities (APIACU) after several years as Acting Executive Director of the Asian Pacific American Institute for Congressional Studies (APAICS). She was appointed by the U.S. President in 1997 to 2001 to be Director of the U.S. Commission on Civil Rights. From 1993 to 1997 Ms. Moy served as the Executive Assistant to the Director of the White House Office of Public Liaison, working in constituency outreach programs and official White House events. Ms. Moy also served as Chief of Staff of Representative Frank Horton (R-NY) from 1973 to 1992, managing the Washington and district offices, overseeing a budget of one million dollars, representing the Congressman in meetings with key Hill Congressmen and women, advising on policy programs, developing legislation, and serving as liaison to members, staff, committees, and constituents. Ms. Moy is thanked by Hon. Frank Horton for her efforts in working with Jeanie Jew to pass legislation recognizing Asian/Pacific American Heritage Week, and now Month. Congressman Horton was the principal sponsor of this legislation in the U.S. Congress. Ms. Moy was his administrative assistant at that time. Moy also served as Chair, Congressional Staff Delegations, to various Asian countries, and as co-founding member of the New York Administrative Assistant Association. She was past National President of the Organization of Chinese American Women. Ms. Moy had several mayoral appointments. She was former Vice Chair and commissioner on Serve D.C. (formerly the D.C. Commission for National and Community Service) and the D.C. Metropolitan Post Standards Board, and D.C. Commission on Women.

She is also Senior Advisor to the U.S.-Asia Foundation; member of the Hawaii State Society, and Secretary and Board member on the National Asian Pacific Center on Aging.

### Rosetta Lai, National President, 2003-2008

Rosetta Lai was the Executive Director of Asian American LEAD (AALEAD), a non-profit organization, which serves the needs of low-income Asian American youth in the Greater DC Region. She is a strong and experienced leader who brings a unique blend of experiences and talent honed throughout her career as a corporate executive, educator and leader in Asian American nonprofit organizations.

Rosetta spent 20 years in the corporate sector holding senior positions with global companies such as Motorola, IBM and NCS/Pearson helping business units improve their organizational effectiveness. Her work took her around the country and the Asia Pacific Region. From 1997 to 2001, she was the Director of Organization Development for Motorola in the Asia Pacific Region headquartered in Singapore and Beijing. During her tenure in Asia Pacific, Rosetta was instrumental in succession planning for all executive positions in the region, helping to ease the transition of local control of the corporation to Asian managers.

Rosetta has applied the results-oriented techniques of corporate management to non-profit organizations when she served as President of the Organization of Chinese Americans (OCA), Chicago Chapter in the 1980s and as the National President of the Organization of Chinese American Women from 2003-2008. In 1987, she was part of the 20 Women Leader Delegation under OCAW's Women to Women Program to visit The People's Republic of China, Taiwan and Hong Kong. She joined AALEAD in 2005 when she moved to Washington, DC and is currently their Executive Director.

Prior to entering the corporate sector, Ms. Lai spent eight years in education where she was the Dean of Women at Lake Forest Academy in Chicago and the Academic Dean at St. Mary's Academy in South Bend, Indiana. She holds an M.S. in Sociology from the University of Notre Dame and a Bachelor of Arts in History from St. Mary's College, both located in Notre Dame, Indiana.

***About AALEAD***

Founded in 1995, AALEAD's overwhelming goal is to increase the opportunities and ability of low-income Asian American children to move out of poverty and become successful, self-sufficient adults. AALEAD firmly believes that education is the key to meeting this goal. However, AALEAD understands that children need additional family, school, and personal supports, not just academic assistance, to succeed. Consequently, AALEAD uses a five-pronged approach to youth development, offering each child after school intervention in a safe space, mentoring, tutoring, family support and educational advocacy. For more information, visit www.aalead.org.

# Appendix 5

## OCAW Guest Writers

### Betty Butz

Betty Butz was born in Guangdong, China, to Dr. and Mrs. Jim Lum, and grew up in Hong Kong. In 1968, she was awarded a full scholarship at International Christian University in Tokyo, Japan, and received a B.A. degree in liberal arts in 1972. She continued her studies in communications at Ohio University, Athens, Ohio, receiving her M.A. degree in 1974.

In 2003, Betty helped to translate and publish a bilingual book titled *Gems in Children's Drawings and Poems*, Varsity Press. She has traveled to many cities in the USA and Asia teaching English, Chinese and Japanese.

Betty's education and experiences prepared her well for civic leadership. For many years she has been active in organizing and leading a variety of clubs. In 2000, she represented Pilot Club International, Singapore Chapter, at an organization conference in Boston, as the chapter President. She is a past President of Ikebana International, New Orleans Chapter, and she has been serving as President of the Organization of Chinese American Women, New Orleans Chapter, since 2008.

After Hurricane Katrina in 2005, Betty and her family chose to stay in New Orleans since the climate, natural environment, plethora of cultural activities, and resilient attitude of the people had become very much part of her life.

## CYNTHIA CHANG

Cynthia Chang has been a member of the Organization of Chinese American Women-Silicon Valley Chapter since 1986, shortly after Dorothy Lee founded this chapter in Silicon Valley, and has stayed actively involved in the chapter to the present time. She served as chapter President from 1991-1993 then again, from 2005-2007.

Besides OCAW-SVC, Cynthia has been actively involved in school and community organizations. She currently serves as board President of Los Gatos-Saratoga High School District and is in her 14th year, since 1998, serving on this board. She also served on Saratoga Union School District as a board member from 1994-1998. As a CPA/ MBA, she is particularly interested in ensuring fiscal responsibility and accountability of the public education system. She has a passion for educating children so they can become ethical, responsible and contributing members of society.

She was a BSA Troop Committee Chair for six years. She also served as Treasurer and a founding board member of the Chinese Historical and Cultural Project which fund-raised and built a Chinese museum then donated it to the city of San Jose. She was also the co-organizer of a Saratoga Rotary-sponsored Building Bridges project which promoted a better understanding of the different cultures and religions in the community.

Cynthia enjoys reading, dancing, modeling and doing Tai-Chi. She also wishes to always keep a smile on her face and spread happiness to all the people she encounters.

## Jean Chen

Born in China and raised in Taiwan, Jean came to the U.S. in 1968 and received a B.A. in Fine Arts from San Francisco State College and a M.F.A. in Advertising Design from Syracuse University.

She had a distinguished career as a Graphic Designer at IBM Research Center in San Jose while raising a family. Upon early retirement, she established a successful second career in Human Resources. Jean officially retired in 2008 after serving as the Director of HR at a South Bay technology company. She feels very fortunate to have experienced both careers and has many fond memories of those times.

Jean loves to give a helping hand and has always been involved in community services. Believing that everyone can make a difference, besides being active in OCAW-Silicon Valley Chapter (OCAW-SVC) functions, she has actively participated in the following organizations: San Jose Chinese School, Shin Shin Educational Foundation, Asian American Community Involvement, Sunnyvale Community Center and the San Jose Museum. She was president of the OCAW-SVC in 1993 and was among its several members who visited OCAW headquarters in what we on the west coast know as Metropolitan Washington, D.C. in 1997.

Jean currently resides in Walnut Creek, California and devotes her time to the arts, music and photography.

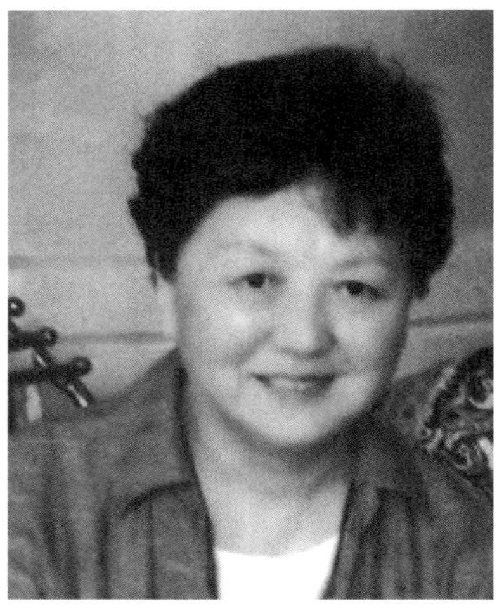

## Lungching Chiao, Ed. D.

Dr. Lungching Chiao is a compassionate educational administrator building bridges between the United States and China through the Education and Science Society, Inc. (ESS) and Support Education in Rural China (SERC), headquartered in Virginia. She is Vice-president of the Board of Directors of ESS and Chairperson of the SERC Executive Committee.

ESS is a non-profit, non-political educational organization, registered as a 501 (C) (3) charitable organization in the State of New York. Its missions are to (1) promote understanding between the peoples of the United States and China and (2) promote human and social development in rural China by raising literary levels and improving the quality of education.

Dr. Chiao received her Doctor of Education degree from the University of Virginia in Education Leadership Foundation and Policy and an Honorary Doctoral Degree from the National University of Chengchi University in Taiwan. Her favorite title, however, is "teacher" or "educator."

## Cynthia Chin-Lee

Cynthia Chin-Lee and her four older siblings were born and raised in Washington, D.C. by a medical doctor father and a homemaker/artist mother. Cynthia began writing for fun when she was in the sixth grade. "I liked writing poetry and scribbling in my journal because I found it comforting and therapeutic. I still write for that reason and because I like playing with words."

Cynthia attended Harvard University where she studied East Asian Languages. She spent her junior year abroad at the Mandarin Training Center of National Taiwan Normal University. After graduating from Harvard *magna cum laude*, Cynthia accepted a graduate fellowship at the East-West Center on the campus of the University of Hawaii in Honolulu, Hawaii.

She began a technical writing career by writing for banks and high-tech companies. She has also written freelance articles for magazines and newspapers, as well as taught writing classes at community colleges and universities. She currently works as a publications manager at Oracle.

Cynthia's first book, *Almond Cookies & Dragon Well Tea* (Polychrome Publishing 1993) is an autobiographical tale of friendship.

She is also the author of *A is For Asia* (Orchard Books 1997), which Ruminator Review called one of the "Best 100 American Children's Books of the Century," and *A is For the Americas* (Orchard Books 1999) which earned an award from the National Council for Social Studies and Children's Books as a Notable Children's Book in Social Studies in 2000 and earned recognition as an Americas Award Commended Book. She has also written *Amelia to Zora: Twenty-six Women Who Changed the World,* and *Akira to Zoltan: Twenty-six Men Who Changed the World* and *Operation Marriage* (Reach and Teach, PM Press).

She is a lifetime OCAW member of the Silicon Valley Chapter and an award winning speaker. She lives in Palo Alto, California with her husband and two children.

## LINDA DEVINE

Linda Devine and her family are one unit. She is 2nd from the left in the family picture. Linda is a Smith College graduate. She is a former State Department Protocol Officer and staff member at the White House and the U.S. International Cultural and Trade Center Presidential Commission. She also served on the Board of Governors of the National Speleological Society and as an officer, board member and trustee of the District of Columbia Grotto, the Potomac Speleological

Club, the Cave Conservancy of The Virginias and the Cave Conservancy Foundation.

She is OCAW Vice-president for Communications and e-Newsletter Editor. Linda and husband Ed, a ship structural engineer, are proud parents of daughter Amanda, a graduate of Dartmouth College, and sons Tommy and Jeremy, currently students at Ohio State University. Linda is very talented and compassionate. Besides being an outdoors person of note and an accomplished writer and editor, she is also a brilliant pianist.

### ANNE HU

Anne Hu, President of OCAW-Silicon Valley Chapter from 2003-2004, is currently on the Board of OCAW-SVC with four other past presidents. She was born in Taiwan and emigrated to San Jose, California when she was 14 years old. She got her first full-time job as a college intern at IBM and later switched her major to Psychology. She holds a B.S. in Psychology from San Jose State University and an Apparel Production certificate from the Fashion Institute of Design and Merchandising.

She is interested in bowling, traveling, reading mystery novels and Toastmasters. A member of Toastmasters since 1995, she mentors new members and provides coaching to high school students on communication and leadership skills.

Anne is currently working for E & E Company as Product Manager. The company is a Home Textile Importer and designs and manufactures for U.S. major retail chains and specialty stores.

## SYBIL KYI

Sybil was born and raised in Hilo, Hawaii, eldest child of the late Kenneth Aloiau Wong and Betsy Nip Wong, eldest grandchild of Chan Poo Nip and Sau Yung Ching Nip and one of many grandchildren of Wong Aloiau (Wong Lo Yau) and Mew Hin Tam Aloiau. Sybil has three daughters and three grandchildren. She is retired from state government service after a career of 42 years.

Sybil graduated from Hilo High School in 1953. Her first two years of college were at Douglass College of Rutgers University. She completed her baccalaureate in Political Science at the University of Michigan in 1957. While working in New York City from 1957-1959, she attended New York University and studied Southeast Asian Studies followed by doing field research in southeast Asia. Upon her return to Hawaii she was employed by the State Department of Labor and Industrial Relations. Subsequent post-graduate studies related to her career field were completed at a summer institute at Claremont College, California in 1968 and in sabbatical studies at UCLA School of Education and School of Business Management in 1977.

She is the 42nd President of the Associated Chinese University Women (ACUW), an organization founded in 1931. She has maintained active leadership in ACUW, serving on the Board of Directors and chairing a variety of committees over these many years.

## DOROTHY LEE

Dorothy Lee, widely known as Doris Lee, is the founder and first President of the Organization of Chinese American Women-Silicon Valley Chapter in 1986. It is commonly known today as OCAW-SVC. She was inspired to start OCAW after hearing a rousing speech by her sister, Esther Lee; then talking with Pauline W. Tsui; and advice from her late mother, Phoebe Chu Lee. The 'fire in my heart' was to urge Chinese Americans to know more about Chinese American history and to participate in mainstream America for all the benefits and opportunities available in education, working opportunities and a peaceful family life and to give back so others can have a good life too.

I was a leader of a computer software team developing systems to build Bradley fighting vehicles. Later I worked as an IT manager. Currently, I am a city commissioner, Purdue University Presidential Council Member and president of many organizations in the Chicago area. Also, I have established several scholarships at Purdue University, my high school and an undergraduate college in Taipei, Taiwan.

### Chelsea Lo

Chelsea Lo is a junior at Barnard College, Columbia University, majoring in economics with a minor in political science. She hopes to pursue international development and the global empowerment of women. She was a summer intern at the Washingtonian Magazine and a news deputy editor and a staff news reporter for the university newspaper. On campus she enjoys singing in an a cappella group, playing an active role in the student Christian community and discovering the many cultural and culinary delights New York has to offer. Her interests also include reading, cooking, fashion and soccer.

### Josephine Lo, Esq.

Josephine Lo, Esq., is a tax partner at the law firm of Pillsbury Winthrop Shaw Pittman. She advises banks, financial institutions and developers involved in affordable housing, historic rehabilitation, community revitalization and economic development projects throughout the United States. She is also familiar with the organization and operation of nonprofit charities, foundations, hospitals and trade associations. She received her J.D., *cum laude*, from Georgetown University, her M.Ed. and M.A. both in counseling psychology from Columbia University and her B.A., *magna cum laude*, in sociology from Mississippi University for Women. She was born and raised in Hong Kong and is fluent in Mandarin and Cantonese. She admires beauty in all forms: in music, character, the English and Chinese languages and women with grace, style and intellect.

## AI-CHU WANG

Ai-chu Wang was born in Taiwan. She came to the United States for graduate school in 1974. She has been working in the financial field since 1988. Her husband, Pong, works in the computer industry. She has a daughter, a son and a three year old granddaughter. They all live in the Bay Area in California. Ai-chu loves dance, music and to travel. She enjoys spending time with family and friends. Ai-chu was President of OCAW-SVC from 2002-2003. Currently, she is a member of the Board of Directors of OCAW-SVC.

## MARGOT WEI

I was born in Beijing, China and finished high school there. My parents, my five siblings and I lived in Beijing during the 1930s when it was under Japanese rule. My father was a Professor and Dean of Arts and Letters at Yenching University and my mother was a Professor of Physical Education at Yenching University. Soon after the Japanese attacked Pearl Harbor in Honolulu, Hawaii, my father was taken as a prisoner by the Japanese and held in prison in Beijing. I remember taking fresh, clean clothes to him every week. I was never able to see or speak to him. I just dropped his clothes off at the prison drop off point and assumed the clothes would get to him.

While in prison and after he died, my mother worked very hard as a Physical Education teacher at Yenching University to raise us six children up, giving us the best that she could and teaching us the important human values so we would be strong, law abiding and do good works for our family and for others.

I came to the United States when I was about 19, having graduated from high school in Beijing, and attended Oberlin College. I majored in Social Work and took a job at St. Barnabas House in New York City, working there for 26 years. Today, that agency is no longer in operation.

I was very active in OCAW programs in its early stages of development. I enjoy Chinese brush painting and took lessons from a famous artist, a personal friend of mine.

I am a proud mother of three girls. Our oldest, a talented and compassionate M.D. in Geriatrics, is deceased. Daughter number two is an engineer and daughter number three is employed at the University of Pennsylvania. I also have nine grandchildren and one great-grandchild. Family means everything to me, and I am sure, others feel the same way too.

### Genevieve Puanani Woo

My wonderful Chinese mother, Lily Kwai Yoke, and her 12 siblings were first born Chinese in Hawaii/America. Her father, from China, was a cook. Her mother came over as a *mui chai*, or slave/maid to work for a local Chinese family. I knew my Apo very well.

I retired in 2004, an educator/administrator for 42 years in Hawaii: 30 years at Kamehameha Schools in Honolulu and 12 years at Waiakea High School in Hilo.

I have project directed 11 books out of 21 books on behalf of a 501(C)(3) organization, the Hawaii Chinese History Center (HCHC), in Honolulu. Seven of those 11 books were produced by the University of Hawaii Press. That seventh book launched in 2009 and concluded with a quick sell-out of 750 books. Lee S. Motteler, Merrilee Holmes, and Sybil Kyi worked with me on that project. Our books were about the history of the Chinese in Hawaii, as part of the history of China, of Hawaii and of the United States of America. I was elected president of HCHC eight consecutive years, an 18 member Board, the only female president and longest serving thus far. We had an active, scholarly Editorial Board.

As project director of this book, *History of the Organization of Chinese American Women*, I wish to acknowledge the detailed advice and technical know-how of Ms. Lucille C. Aono, production editor and her staff at the University of Hawai'i Press and again to Lee S. Motteler, copy editor and Merrilee Holmes, photo editor. The Advisors/editors were Yeu-Tsu Margaret Lee, M.D., Sybil Kyi, Linda Devine and Cynthia Chin-Lee. Bertram S. Y. Mao wrote the calligraphy for the cover of the book.

I extend my deep respect and gratitude to each guest writer: Betty Butz, Cynthia Chang, Jean Chen, Lungching Chiao, Ed. D., Cynthia Chin-Lee, Linda Devine, Anne Hu, Florence Kwok, Sybil Kyi, Dorothy Lee, Chelsea Lo, Josephine S. Lo, Esq., Ai-chu Wang, Margot Wei and Margaret Wu.

The OCAW national leaders, Pauline W. Tsui, Ambassador Julia Chang Bloch, Hon. Lily Lee Chen, Lily K. Lai, Ph.D., Faith Lee Breen, Ph.D., Jeanie F.L. Jew and Rosetta Lai wrote wide and deep.

Thank you all for writing your story about OCAW.

## Margaret Wu

Margaret Wu graduated from the National Taiwan University and received a Scottish Rites Free Masons scholarship to pursue her graduate study in accounting at George Washington University. She spent the first half of her career in public accounting and the second half in overseeing the accounting systems and finances of two companies. She has made the Washington, D.C. area her home for fifty plus years and loves its wonderful natural and cultural environments.

# APPENDIX 6

## OCAW HISTORY BOOK DONORS

### RUTH HOW KUO, 1901-2005

A pioneer of her time, Mrs. Kuo, a graduate of the New England Conservatory of Music in Boston, taught piano for many years in both China and the United States. A woman for all seasons, she was a Founding Member of the Organization of Chinese American Women; a Co-founder of the Hwasheng Chorus; Treasurer of the Sino-American Cultural Society in Washington, D.C.; and President of the London Chinese Women's Club in London.

Her husband, Dr. Ping Wen Kuo, was the founder and founding president of Southeastern University in Nanking and Cai-Jing University in Shanghai, China.

A strong supporter of OCAW's programs, Mrs. Kuo's early contribution established OCAW's scholarships for its annual Presidential Classroom Program in 1989. Later, her generous donations were made for OCAW's annual Rural Scholarships for Middle School Girls in China; music fellowships for young artists in the U.S.; the U.S./China Education Trust's College Scholarships in China; Asian American Leadership after school programs for needy youths and families in Washington, D.C., Maryland and Virginia; and the Hepatitis B Initiatives for minorities in Metropolitan Washington, D.C.

OCAW deeply appreciates Mrs. Kuo's decades of generosity.

## Edward Y. Fu

Ed Fu, a native of Washington, D.C. is the son of Anming and Shuili Fu. He attended Wilson High School and George Washington University in the District of Columbia. After working at the U.S. Department of Labor, he founded a consulting firm. His firm, Fu Associates, in operation since 1980, employs approximately 75 people and provides large scale database analyses for government agencies. OCAW appreciates his warm support for making this book a reality.